SGAA
REFERENCE & TECHNICAL MANUAL

A COMPREHENSIVE GUIDE TO STAINED GLASS

SECOND EDITION • SECOND PRINTING

THE STAINED GLASS ASSOCIATION OF AMERICA
STAINED GLASS SCHOOL

THE STAINED GLASS ASSOCIATION OF AMERICA

Raytown, MO

Chapter 21
Lighting

Disclaimer:

This manual is designed to provide accurate and authoritative information in regard to the subject matter covered. It is issued with the understanding that the publisher and The Stained Glass Association of America Stained Glass School are not engaged in rendering legal, accounting, or any professional advice whatsoever. If expert advice or legal assistance is required, the services of a competent professional person should be sought.

The viewpoints expressed herein are those of the authors and not necessarily those of The Stained Glass Association of America or its members. Please note that laws and procedures are constantly changing and are subject to differing interpretations. It is the responsibility of the reader and user of this manual to check all material before relying on it. Neither the publisher nor The Stained Glass Association of America Stained Glass School makes any guarantees concerning the information in this Manual or the use to which it is put. No liability whatsoever is assumed for any inaccuracies or errors, although any communication relating thereto would be appreciated.

This reprinting is not an updated edition. For the latest information on safety in the studio or the current standards for stained glass restoration, the reader is encouraged the obtain *Recommendations for Studio Safety* and *The Standards and Guidelines for the Preservation of Historic Stained Glass*, both of which are available from the SGAA Headquarters by calling 800.438-9581 or visiting

PREFACE TO THE SECOND PRINTING

Welcome to the second printing of the *SGAA Reference & Technical Manual, Second Edition.*

In the original printing of this edition, the entire manual was published as one leather-bound volume. In this second printing, the book will be broken up and reprinted chapter-by-chapter over a period of several years. Each chapter will appear in the reprint exactly as it did in the original printing of the second edition.

As there have been no copies of the last printing available for some time now, the Stained Glass Association of America hopes this reprinting will help to fill a void in available technical information regarding stained glass. Be aware that this reprinting is not an updated edition and that for the latest information on safety in the studio or the current standards for stained glass restoration, the reader is encouraged the obtain *Recommendations for Studio Safety* and *The Standards and Guidelines for the Preservation of Historic Stained Glass*, both of which are available from the SGAA Headquarters by calling 800.438-9581 or visiting *www.stainedglass.org.*

Over the coming months, additional chapters will be made available again. Not all of the book will be reprinted; some of the chapters are too out-of-date and describe processes no longer considered safe or for which the materials described are no longer available. However, the majority of the *SGAA Reference & Technical Manual, Second Edition* will once again be made available to the stained glass practitioner. Watch *www.stainedglass.org*, the *Kaleidoscope* and, of course, The *Stained Glass* Quarterly for updates as this project progresses and more chapters become available.

Richard Gross
Editor & Media Director,
Stained Glass Association of America

SGAA REFERENCE & TECHNICAL MANUAL
A COMPREHENSIVE GUIDE TO STAINED GLASS

COMPLETE TABLE OF CONTENTS

Part 1
Historical

Part 2
Glass

Part 3
Principles and Considerations
of Stained Glass Fabrication

Part 4
Procedures of Glass Fabrication

Part 5
Surface Treatments

Part 6

General Procedures

Chapter 21

Lighting for Stained Glass

*Paul Crist, Alastair Duncan, Saara Gallin, Dale Howard,
Carole Perry, Douglas Phillips and Mona Phillips*

Table of Contents

Chapter 21
Lighting for Stained Glass

Table of Contents

Chapter 21
Lighting for Stained Glass

Table of Contents

A. Color and Light in Interior Spaces
Saara Gallin

Light is the symbol of the divine. With the exception of the flickering flame of a candle, nowhere is this more evident than in the relationship between light and stained glass. The interaction of the color in stained glass with light is unwritten music. Consequently, discussions of color in stained glass must simultaneously consider its relationship with light. One without the other is like a musical score never being heard—without sound, without appreciation. Thorn Prikker once made the comment that stained glass is painting with light. I think of my work as sculpting with light.

Can stained glass have magic without the existence of natural light? I think so. The beauty of glass lies in its relationship with light. My present concern is with glass in interior spaces, the lighting for which is seldom natural. Yet the non-existence of natural light by no means precludes the aesthetic wonder of glass magic. In interiors, what should be considered is the nature and direction of the light as well as the type of glass to be used. For example, opalescent glass survives the harshness of incandescent and fluorescent light more easily than does pot metal glass. However, my focus is on pot metal glass. mouth-blown glass)

What happens if one persists in attempting to use pot metal glass in an interior situation? For one thing, all of the subtlety of the glass can be destroyed by the harsh light. The magic is gone. If one continues to persist, what possibilities exist? Clear glass and tints always seem to work with low levels of ambient light, which seems to us the average situation in interior spaces; however, the darker, more powerful, sensual colors are not turned on by soft light, and the subtle textures and optics of hand-blown glass are usually destroyed by strong transmitted light.

A ploy that works especially well with clear glass and light tints in a situation where minimal light is available is to use mirror behind the work of pot metal glass. A space of two and one half to five inches between the mirror and the glass is desirable. Careful choice of pale tints, with an emphasis on the texture rather than color, will work to offset the tendency to 'glitziness' inherent in this situation. The light in the room will go through the pale tints, bounce against the mirror and return to activate the glass. I have used this successfully in a number of situations where I was preparing to tell the client that perhaps he did not really want glass, but should look to other materials.

I believe that one of the major reasons underlying the poor acceptance by galleries of non-commissioned stained glass is that galleries, by their very nature, are *interior* spaces. Only on rare occasions is there much window space. When the work is shown, it is most often exhibited with a very poor understanding of what can be done with the existing light situation. The best resolution to this persistent problem is to ensure that the gallery lights, which are usually in the ceiling, are directed towards a white wall. The glass is then hung with a good space between it and the wall. The lights are between the glass and the wall. To repeat the order a different way:

1. The viewer
2. The glass
3. The space and light and, finally,
4. The wall.

The balance of light must always be such that there is more light on the side of the glass away from the viewer. Ugly hot spots of light are avoided in this way, and the pot metal glass is not drowned in a sea of bad light.

What do you do when existing ceiling lights are in the wrong place? A recent innovative and successful use of light was developed in attempting to mount a temporary exhibition of modern non-commissioned stained glass in connection with an exhibit, 'The Great Windows of New Rochelle.'

Lighting was rented for the occasion from a firm that provides theatre lighting. The lights were placed on the floor and were directed up at the white walls. The walls were easily washed with light, with no hot spots. The intensity of light was adjusted with reference to the needs of a specific work from a central control panel placed out of sight.

The ability to use pot metal glass in interior installations without destroying the very essence which makes it so wonderful to work with is a current reality. Low voltage halogen light is being used more and more by galleries and interior design people. They are increasingly aware of this light's ability to make all art work glow. This is particularly true of stained glass. The light is extraordinary. Once you have worked with it, it is hard to settle for anything else. Remember the basic rule: the preponderance of light must be on the side of the glass away from the viewer, with halogen light as with all others.

The contribution of low voltage halogen light to the interior use of stained glass is that all the colors and textures are true and never obliterated. The possibilities for the use of pot metal glass—in conjunction with this modern gift of light—in homes, offices, and restaurants are endless. Of course, as wonderful as it is, low voltage halogen light can never compete with natural light, light that changes the work from morning to evening and from season to season. Nevertheless, the faerie-like, magic-creating, aesthetic-inducing qualities of glass can be used within interior spaces and can be used effectively.

B. Artificial Lighting of Stained Glass Panels
Douglas Phillips with Mona Phillips

When we think of lighting for stained glass, we need to remind ourselves that stained glass is ordinarily seen by looking through the glass at a lighted background. This can be sky, foliage, or buildings. Such background images, dimly seen through the stained glass and distorted by its texture, create the familiar 'glassy' look. For best viewing conditions, the brightest light should be on the side of the glass opposite the viewer; however, we do not want the light source to be seen through the glass. For example, we notice how sunlight, when it shines directly through stained glass, can create uncomfortable and distracting glare. Uncontrolled light can be disastrous.

Our aim in lighting stained glass should be to provide a lighted background using a hidden source of light. How we accomplish this depends on how the stained glass will be displayed.

If the glass is in a window opening, we may need to provide lighting that enables viewing at night, from either the outside or the inside. In many instances, glass may be set not in a window opening but rather against a lighted wall or in a box that functions both as frame and light source—a 'light box.' We use various lighting techniques in our installations and there are underlying principles for each approach to the lighting of stained glass; however it should be remembered that lighting itself is also an art, and these principles serve only as guides.

Stained glass installations projecting very far into a room could be awkward or hazardous. Thus, light boxes or wall-backed displays are often limited to a depth of no more than six or seven inches. This narrow depth creates problems in illumination.

We recommend that light boxes be constructed with a frame, six to seven inches wide around the perimeter of the glass opening. Fluorescent tubes to illumine the glass are shielded and concealed by this frame.

Depending on the size of the panel, it can be lit with side lamps alone or may also need tubes at top and bottom. To a distance of approximately 30″, the beam spread from these tubes will meet in the middle of the glass panel to produce a relatively uniform illumination. With larger panels, the fluorescent beams will weaken toward the center. We could improve the spread by increasing the depth of the light box, but the light would still weaken with distance, and in most situations a deeper light box would be undesirable.

With greater width in the stained glass area and the same limited depth in the space behind it, we must put fluorescent lamps directly behind the stained glass for illumination. If we do not, we will have light at the sides (or ends) and not in the middle.

We have said that one basic principle is that the source of light must be hidden. In order to hide fluorescent tubes placed behind stained glass, we insert a diffusing panel *between* the tubes and the glass; ⅛″ white translucent acrylic makes an effective diffusing panel but there is a trade-off. In return for shielding the light source, we lose

some of the glassy effect we wish. We can compensate for this by adding texture or some variation to the diffusing panel.

The fluorescent tube we prefer is the GE Chroma 50. It has a color temperature of 5000 and projects a light that approximates a mixture of sunlight and sky. The light is white enough to bring out the full color spectrum of the stained glass and yet has a touch of the warmth we associate with a sunny day. (In fact the color temperature of a sunny day, noon sunlight, is rated at 4870K.)

Other types of fluorescent lamps with good color rendering capabilities are those in the GE Specification Series. The ones with moderate color temperature values such as the GE SPX35 at 3500 Kelvins have long life as well as a good Color Rendering Index Value of 82. They also have a high luminous efficiency.

The higher color rendering index alone, does not however, mean the more pleasant or desirable light. A cool lamp and a warm lamp both may have the same coloring index rating, but the glass colors will not look the same. One usually will be preferred over the other depending on the intent of the artist or taste of the viewer.

Beyond the basic principles, much that is involved in lighting stained glass is both subjective and creative. If you, as the artist, are lighting your own work, the question is how you want your work to be perceived. If you are a lighting designer, the intent of the artist must be taken into consideration in the lighting of the work.

Different looks may be achieved with various light intensities and lamp colors. Advertising material from the manufacturers of these lamps usually has charts in color showing the precise area of the color spectrum produced by their product. These are available at no charge.

As the artist, it would be perfectly feasible to use a lower color temperature lamp to warm a cool composition. The lower (warmer) color temperature lamps also could be used to emphasize the reds, oranges and yellows in another design. Similarly, a cooler lamp might be used for the opposite reasons—to cool a too hot panel, or to bring out the blues and greens.

For example, stained glass that our studio installed in a light box in a dining room at the GE Lighting Institute, Nela Park, Ohio, has a dual lighting system with dimmers. Because of this variable quality in light, we recommend the installation of dimmers in every electrical lighting system for stained glass.

There is one fluorescent light system at 5000K to relate to daylight viewing and another at 2000K to relate to nighttime, incandescent lamps. The cooler rays of the higher temperature lamp bring out the blues and reds, while the lower temperature emphasizes the yellows and oranges. This arrangement corresponds to the natural changing conditions of daylight and creates different moods.

In another instance, we were called in by a collector of Tiffany windows to evaluate the lighting system he had installed, which featured unshielded, tinted incandescent lights directly behind the glass. This lighting, although counter to some of our basic principles, created such a beautiful effect that we left it in place. Tiffany would have loved it! Of course, it was the extreme density of Tiffany's glass that made this an effective solution.

We seek an even white light because generally it brings out all the color and subtleties of the stained glass design as we, the artists, intended. However, in the same sense that daylight has different colors and intensities, the lighting for stained glass can and should be used as an element in the design. Light can enhance strengths or compensate for weaknesses in the design. We can paint with light, especially with the use of incandescent floodlights and spotlights. The GE Wattmizer II Halogen PAR Flood is an excellent lamp we have used successfully.

When fluorescent tubes are directly behind the stained glass, proper spacing is essential for even illumination. The distance from the top of the lamp to the stained glass multiplied by 1.5 gives the proper distance between fluorescent lamps on centers. This is the proper geometric ratio for even light distribution, 1 by 1.5. Of course it will still be necessary to use a diffusing panel between the glass and lights unless the glass has enough opacity and density to create its own diffusion.

When space permits the work to be mounted as much as several feet from a wall, we can mount floodlights or spotlights for particularly effective lighting treatments. Again, these lights should always be recessed or hidden. Our studio had an exciting commission that involved such parameters. We were asked to design a 20 X 14 ½' floor-to-ceiling reredos, a screen of stained glass, to be installed in front of a blank wall in a chapel at the Lutheran Home in Westlake, Ohio. See *Figure 20.1.*

Since we wished the screen to be visible from all angles, we curved it, starting from the wall at one end of its 20' length, bowing out to 30" at the center, then returning to the wall at the other end. The wall became the chord of a stained glass arc.

We chose the GE Precise Multi-Mirror®, low voltage quartz halogen lamp to light the wall, because of its small size (2") and because the faceted reflector gave us control of the beam spread through various lamp models. A small-sized fixture made it possible to mount the lamps on the frame unobtrusively at the junction of the mullions and the mutins. The transformers were remote, away from the screen.

We best perceive stained glass by looking through the glass at a lighted something, so we painted a subtle abstract mural on the wall. Its value and hue were sufficient to influence the perception to get that glassy feel but not enough to alter the design of the stained glass.

We aimed the lights at the wall so that the beams crossed each other and painted the wall with an even illumination. Since we knew the beam 'spread' from the product material furnished to us by the General Electric Co., we were able to plot all this on paper before the installation.

In this instance, the combination of small size, whiter light because of the quartz halogen bulb (we liked the color of the light at 3100K), low voltage for long life and increased lumens per watt efficiency, all made the Precise lamp an ideal choice for the setting.

Any large screen must incorporate some means of access to the back for servicing the lamps. The Lutheran Home screen has a door. In other large screens we have used removable panels, sliding panels on tracks, or panels on hinges. In one instance an entire 10' x 14' window was backlighted and hinged; it was so heavy a wheel/caster was installed so it would roll open, like a gate. (See *Figures 21.2–21.5*)

The small size of low voltage halogen lamps makes them practical for light boxes as well as screens. The owners of one of our stained glass panels is refitting the box with a row of tiny halogen lamps on either side for greater light intensity.

Our principles, extended, apply equally well to lighting stained glass windows that are to be viewed from the outside of a building at night. We can consider that we simply have a large light box behind the window, which can be a room, a hall, or an auditorium in the building. The concept applies equally well to religious, commercial, and residential situations.

At Parma United Methodist Church, in Parma, Ohio, there is a large window (approximately 17' by 15') above the entrance. The original night lighting system, floodlights mounted on beams and aimed at the windows, was ineffective. The readily visible sources of light created hot spots.

Our solution was to mount GE Quartzline® floodlights under the window, aimed away from it to illuminate the adjacent walls and ceiling. Since the window is above eye level, the lights are not seen. The variation in lighting reflectance from walls and ceiling related to the variations we find in the everyday viewing of stained glass.

We have used this same approach in similar situations. We remove the offending light fixtures aimed at the stained glass and visible to the viewer. We mount floods under the window or at the sides and aim them away from the window to illumine whatever there is beyond the opening.

While most of our lighting systems are designed for a relatively even level of illumination, this is not an absolute requirement. When lighting either our own work or that of others, we try to illumine all areas of the stained glass equally so as not to emphasize any area of the work over another. The artist has created his or her own emphasis in color and movement; however, completely flat lighting is not necessary or desirable. An unevenness in light can augment and accent the design. This variation should be a matter of design and not of accident.

We designed two slightly curved screens for Agudath Bnai Israel in Lorain, Ohio. (See *Figure 21.06*) Each was 65 by 14', floor to ceiling, and they flanked both sides of the sanctuary, thus isolating it from the straight walls and creating two passageways of varying dimensions along the sides. There were no windows, and the passage had to be kept clear for members of the congregation, who used it to get to their seats through openings in the screen.

Our solution was to mount light fixtures in the ceiling on tracks and aim GE PAR® (parabolic aluminized reflector) flood lamps at the brick walls away from the stained glass. The bricks in the wall were chosen with their degree of reflectance in mind. The light beams were aimed and adjusted to bring out areas of emphasis in the design. The deliberate unevenness created visual excitement and brought out the intent of the design. The light itself created interesting patterns that harmonized with the stained glass design. We literally painted the wall with light.

Seeing color is subjective. Although fluorescent lamps are the most efficient (25%+ light energy produced versus 10-15% for incandescent) and can achieve the highest number on the Color Rendering Index scale, incandescent light is considered the 'norm' or the familiar in terms of color rendering and as a white light source. People are accustomed, through decades of use, to seeing how things look under incandescent light. We have used incandescent lamps very successfully for many years in illuminating stained glass.

The types of incandescent lamps we favor are the GE PAR low voltage lamps, the GE Quartzline® lamp, the Quartzline Halogen lamp, and the Precise® Multi-Mirror Low voltage Halogen lamp. We have used both spots and floods, depending on our requirements. All of these lamps are in the moderate range of 3000K to 4000K. Since the eye cannot distinguish a difference of less than 200K in chromaticity, there is always some flexibility in the choice of lamp whether incandescent or fluorescent is used. The choice of lamp depends on beam projection and spread relative to the space to be lighted. Specific details of beam spread and projection are available from the manufacturer.

Lighting stained glass to be viewed from the inside at night is more difficult. The interior is usually lit to some degree so that we are apt to have competing electrical lighting systems. A bright sunny day might give us 10,000 foot candles on a horizontal surface, a cloudy day, 900. A brightly lit office might have 250 to 300 foot candles at a maximum. It is apparent that achieving a daylight effect at night is extremely difficult if not impossible.

Again, the basic principle is to light something *beyond* the window for the congregation to view. This can be adjacent buildings, trees, or the most effective, a movable screen that could be lighted at night. Attempts to mount light on poles and trees have proven to be ineffective when the lights are aimed at the windows. In one instance, with the cooperation of the Cleveland Electric Illuminating Co., we aimed large searchlights at the windows from the outside. There were beautiful patterns on the ceiling but the reading of the stained glass design left much to be desired.

The only exception to the rule occurs when the glass itself has a diffusing quality as in the Tiffany window we mentioned. Tests we have made show that opalescent glass and some of the older heavily painted windows can be lighted effectively at night from the outside with lights aimed directly at the window.(Trinity Cathedral, Cleveland, OH, 1971.) In essence, the glass is its own diffusing screen. A caution, however: even heavily painted glass has areas where the paint is thin or where there is more transparency. Tests would certainly have to be made before installing any lighting system. In fact, aside from light boxes and minimum space requirements where there is a specific geometry, we recommend field testing before making any installation whether interior or exterior. Many years ago, when we first started investigating lighting for stained glass, lighting engineers could calibrate the basic footcandles needed based on the area to be lighted but we found that field testing was necessary for complete information and satisfactory results.

Our experience confirms the basic lighting concepts:

1. That lighting system is best when the light source is hidden and the space on the opposite side of the glass from the viewer is lighted. Light directed toward the stained glass is ineffective.

2. When the light source is within the viewer's sightline, a diffusing panel of white acrylic should be used to shield the lights. When a diffusing panel is not practical, as when general lighting or light fixtures are visible, the problem can be minimized by floodlighting the adjacent areas and painting them with highly reflective paint. This is particularly important with today's contemporary, more transparent glass.

3. Careful variation and unevenness in the lighting system and in the values and colors of the background surfaces can give a 'glassy' feeling and depth to stained glass that approximates the effect of natural light.

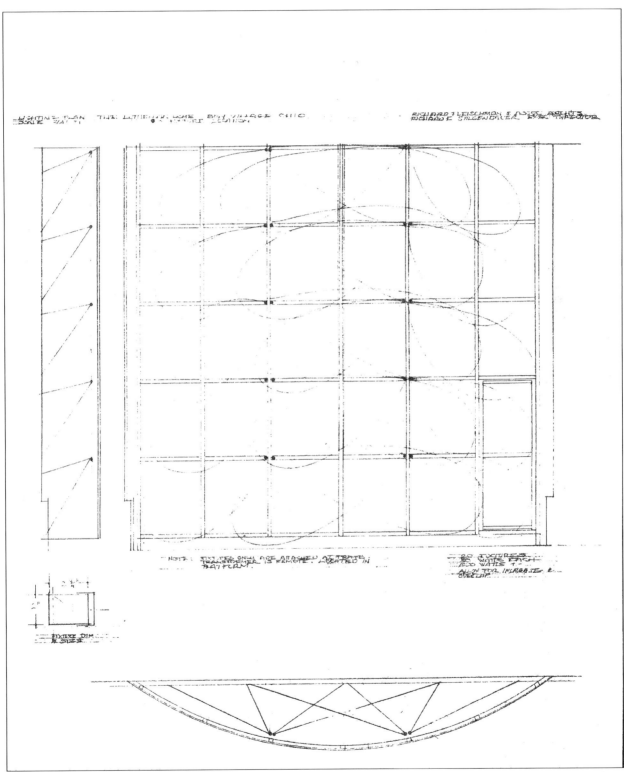

Diagram 21.1: Lighting Plan for The Lutheran Home, Westlake, OH. Fixtures only are attached at frame, transformer is remote, located in platform.

20 Fixtures, 50 Watts each, 1,000 Watts ±, Allow for increase and overlap.

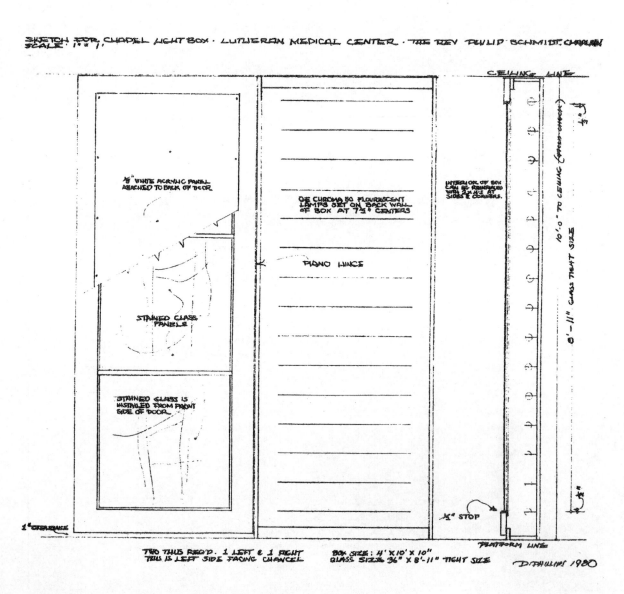

Diagram 21.2: Sketch for Chapel Lightbox, Lutheran Medical Center,
Cleveland, OH.

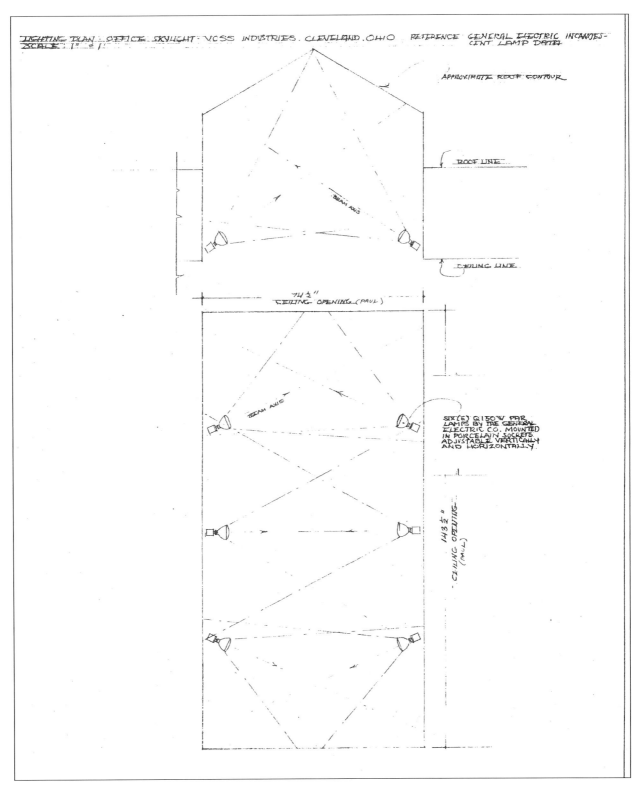

*Diagram 21.3: Lighting Plan. Office Skylight, Voss Industries,
Cleveland, Ohio*

553

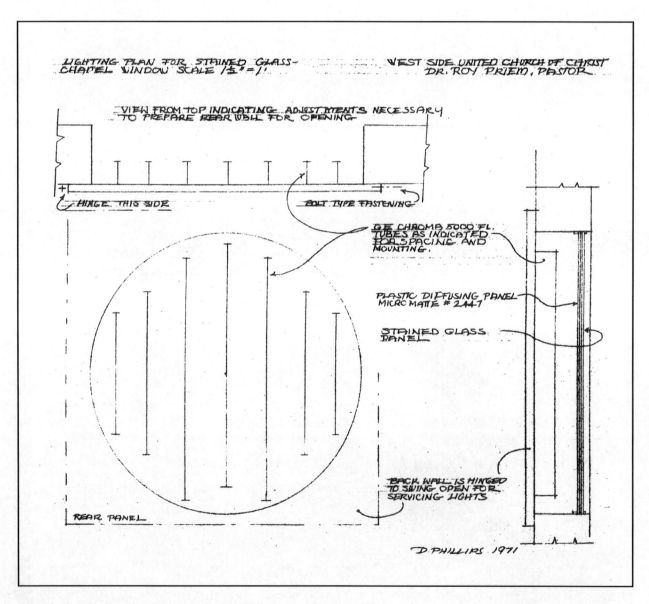

Diagram 21.4: Lighting Plan for Stained Glass, West Side United Church of Christ, Cleveland, OH.

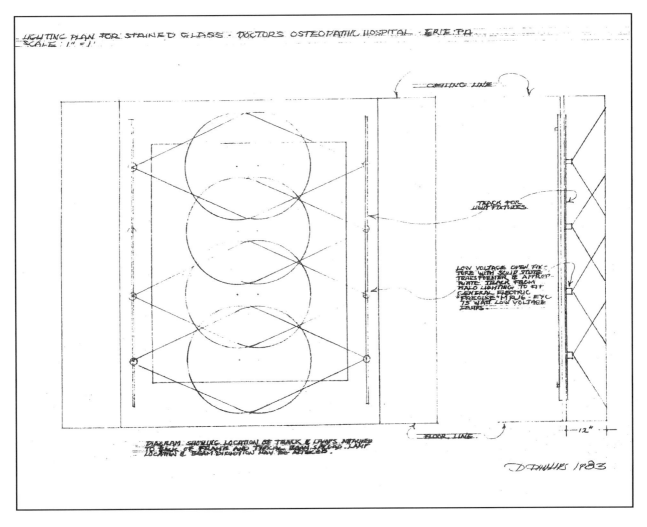

Diagram 21.5: Lighting Plan for Stained Glass. Doctor's Osteopathic Hospital, Erie, PA. Diagram showing location of track and lamps attached to back of frame and typical BGAM Spread. Lamp location and beam direction may be altered.

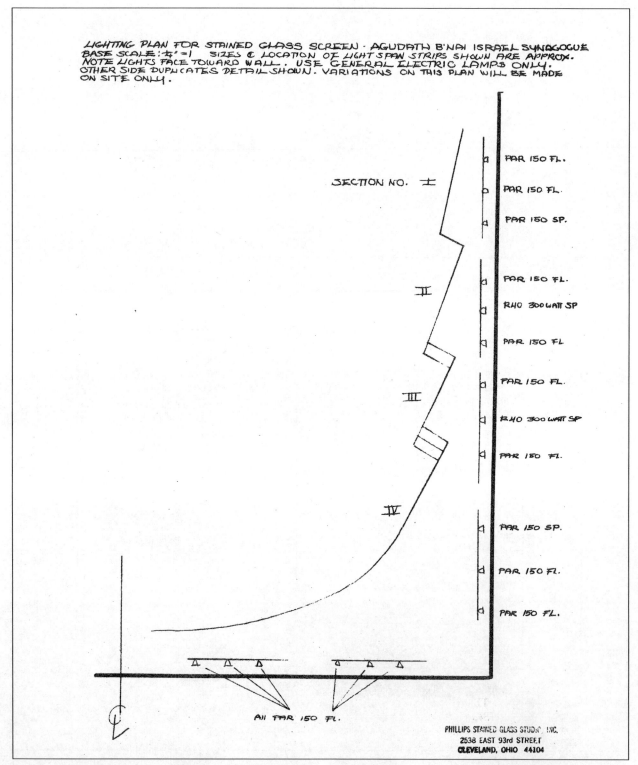

Diagram 21.6: Lighting Plan for stained glass screen. Agudath B'nai Israel Synagogue, Lorrain, OH. Sizes and location of light span strips shown are approx. Note lights face toward wall. Use General Electric Lamps only. Other side duplicates detail shown. Variations on this plan will be made on site only.

C. Lamps

Dale Howard, Paul Crist and Alastair Duncan
Illustrations by David Schlicker

1. Introduction

With the explosion of the crafts movement during the past two decades, it has become somewhat difficult to provide a concise definition of a stained glass lamp. Besides the Art Nouveau creations of the early twentieth century we now have light sculpture, fused glass shades, neon, and low voltage halogen fixtures utilizing asymmetrical stained glass components and idiosyncratic construction techniques. The most appropriate approach for the technical manual seems to be to include comprehensive instruction for the construction of a stained glass lampshade utilizing a lamp mold or form and copper foil. Although narrow in focus, a thorough knowledge of the basics will provide a knowledge and understanding for the construction of a durable, safe work of art.

This chapter is not intended as a comprehensive encyclopedia providing information about all methods of lamp construction. It is assumed that you already have a working knowledge of glass cutting, copper foiling and soldering. (*See Other Chapters*) There is no information provided for the construction of lamps using panel construction or lead came. There are numerous commercial publications with extensive information on the subject. (*Refer to Bibliography*) Although the construction of a lampshade utilizing a lamp form is complex, it is helpful to remember that your complicated project is made one piece at a time, one step at a time, and you will be rewarded for your patience and persistence.

2. History
Alastair Duncan (Reprinted by Permission)

Art Nouveau, which began in England but was to reach its zenith in France, was an ornamental style in which the intention was to capture the quintessence of nature in its every form. Everything had to depict the undulating and biomorphic shapes and lines of flowers and plants. The movement started in the 1870s and reached its full momentum at the turn of the century (often, in fact, termed as fin-de-siecle art), generating some of the finest art the world has ever seen, and leading, as far as we are concerned, to a resurgence in the use of leaded glass as a decorative art form, but with one important difference: that it was for the first time effectively incorporated into three-dimensional form. That this happened is due in part to, first, Swan's (1878), and then Edison's (1879), inventions of the incandescent filament bulb, which they showed independently at the great Paris Universal Exhibition in 1889. Up to this stage, lighting was provided primarily by liquid fuels and by gas, both of which had limiting design constraints. The functional requirements

for liquid fuels, such as methylated spirits and paraffin, were that lamps had to be easily accessible so that they could be refilled regularly, that they always be placed in a strictly upright position, and that they have a protective cover and a fuel reservoir.

Gas, on the other hand, although giving a good incandescent light, has to be in a fixed position and attached to a pipe which, although it could be somewhat disguised, spoiled the appearance of chandeliers and wall-lamps. The above were factors that had obviously limited the design aspects of lamps up to that time.

With the advent of the electric light, the safety considerations which had affected all forms of combustion lighting disappeared, and lamps no longer had to be vertical. This allowed the Art Nouveau modernists to turn their creative talents to the new design possibilities of lighting.

Galle, Lalique, and the Daum brothers in France, Tiffany in the United States, and several other 'leading lights' designed and created glass lampshades which, while faithfully adhering to the stylistic traits of Art Nouveau, made full allowance of the new-found freedom in innovation that the electric light afforded.

All these artists worked with blown glass (examples of which are on permanent display at the Musee des Arts Decoratifs at the Louvre and are well worth seeing), but it was Tiffany who diversified to develop a method of producing machine-made glass in flat form. Because the traditional method of using strips of lead came was too unwieldy, Tiffany incorporated copper foil to bond pieces of glass together. This allowed him to use flat glass to make curved lampshades. It was Tiffany, therefore, who was the founding father of leaded glass in three-dimensional form.

1848, the year that spawned so much revolution throughout the world, was to see the birth of someone who was to revolutionize the world of glass: Louis C. Tiffany. Tiffany was the son of the most fashionable American jeweller, and whose shop, Tiffany and Company, still exists on Fifth Avenue, New York (it opened a branch in Regent Street, London, in 1868). He spurned his father's offer of a place in the firm, however, opting rather for an independent life in the decorative arts, and he was one of the first to be drawn to Europe by the reputation of William Morris.

Tiffany showed a remarkable versatility throughout his artistic career, using numerous different materials to produce a wide range of objects d'art, but he is remembered primarily for his lampshades and, more specifically, for the unique glass with which they were made.

Tiffany's search for a new kind of glass had stemmed from his dissatisfaction with the coloured glass in America at that time: the largely monochromatic, transparent variety used in stained glass windows. Multi-coloured effects could be obtained only by the juxtaposition of the pieces and, in many instances, by the addition of paints and stains. There were three reasons Tiffany found this inadequate for his needs: Firstly, for an adherent of Art Nouveau style, the monochromatic character of the glass was untrue of life, since nothing in nature is uniform in colour; secondly, the application of paint interfered with the transmission of light, one of the principal functions of glass; and thirdly, the glass lacked the innate properties of iridescence and radiance that he desired.

After innumerable experiments, he finally obtained the correct chemical interaction and, in 1881, acquired the patent of an iridescent glass. This was followed by more experimenting to perfect the method of creating multi-coloured, opalescent glass, and his efforts were rewarded in 1894 when a further patent was granted for his Favrile glass. The word Favrile derives from the old English fabrile meaning 'handmade,' which he changed to Favrile to create a unique word for the trademark of his Tiffany Glass and Decorating Company, which he had established in Corona, New York.

That the name Tiffany is now generally used to describe all leaded glass lampshades is a tribute to his monolithic influence on this art form, but it is, in effect, a backhanded compliment as nobody else has ever managed to match his creative brilliance in glass and lampmaking. Anyone who has had the opportunity to see an original Tiffany will appreciate just what it is that made his work unique. On the one hand, his glass was impregnated with a special combination of metallic pigments often in striation or mottle form, which, although sometimes fairly flat in colour when viewed in reflected light, would come alive in transmitted light, being variously kaleidoscopic, incandescent, or phosphorescent. Added to which, the glass with which he worked was often textured in nodular, rippled or fibrillated form to create extraordinary light refractive effects.

In addition, his designs were singularly his own. Not only did he incorporate the prevailing Art Nouveau style into his work to produce floral lamps such as the tulip, apple blossom, jonquil, and poinsettia designs, but he also made a variety of geometrically shaped shades. Between the two—his glass and designs—his work has remained unparalleled to this day.

Art Nouveau, like Baroque and Rococo before it, was in its turn to be replaced, this time by such art movements as surrealism, Art Deco, and the Bauhaus, and it has only recently undergone a renewed popularity. Tiffany, whose work until 5 years ago had seemed destined largely to the world of the museum and the antiquarian, is suddenly back in fashion, and prices of his lamps have consequently skyrocketed. A Tiffany Wisteria lamp which, for example, sold originally for $400.00 in 1906, was auctioned at Sotheby Parke Bernet in New York in 1974 for $42,000 *(and $500,000 in 1989—ed.)*

The revived public interest in Tiffany in America has contributed, in part, to the renaissance that the craft of leaded glass is experiencing at this moment. Not only are Art Nouveau styled lamps being made by professionals and amateurs alike, but the craft has diversified to incorporate innumerable other forms of both two and three-dimensional glass: free-form objects, sculpture, plant holders, mirrors, room dividers, etc. The craft has, in fact, exploded into a boom industry! We are on the threshold of a new, and very distinct, chapter in the history of glass, one which is drawing on both traditional and contemporary art styles to make the craft really eclectic for the first time ever. An exciting range of old and new floral and geometric designs are being reproduced in glass, and as far as style is concerned, anything goes, and often with bewildering effectiveness.

3. Construction of Stained Glass Lamps
Dale Howard and Paul Crist

a. Choice of Project

As mentioned in the introduction, lamp construction is an involved process. Unfortunately the first step, choice of a project, is one of the most difficult. If this is your first copper foiled lamp, it is advised that you consider supervision by an experienced stained glass instructor. As a general rule, the difficulty of lamp construction is related to the number of glass pieces in the lamp; most descriptions of lamp patterns disclose the number of pieces. Although there is an appearance of simplicity, lamps using extensive geometric grids are quite formidable because of the need for precise cutting and fabrication to keep all the grid lines straight. It is suggested that your first lamp be a simple one of 400—600 pieces. Save your dream lamp for your second or third project.

Unless you decide to construct your own design and lamp form, you will be choosing from one of the molds offered by the four companies manufacturing lamp systems. These manufacturers and their addresses are listed below. By contacting these companies or visiting a retail stained glass supplier you may review the catalogs of each.

b. Lamp Mold Manufacturers

H. L. Worden Company
P. O. Box 519
Granger, WA 98932
(800) 54 1-1103

Odyssey
P. O. Box 1876
La Mirada, CA 90637
(800) 228-2631

Studio Design (Rainbow)
49 Shark River Road
Neptune, NJ 07753
(201) 922-1090

Whittemore Durgin Glass Company
Box 2065
Hanover, MA 02339
(800) 262-1790

In the preparation of this chapter each of the listed manufacturers was contacted and asked to provide catalog and instruction materials. A brief description of each system was extracted from the material provided. The intent of this review is to provide information about each lamp system rather than to promote any particular one.

(1) Odyssey System:

Each lamp mold kit contains one full 360° fiberglass form which is dimensionally stable but is not perfectly rigid. The lamp pattern is permanently incised onto the mold. There are currently 60+ precise Tiffany reproductions available and two Art Nouveau designs. The Odyssey kit also contains one Mylar® cutting pattern, a paper pattern used for reference, and a 25 page instruction manual. The Mylar® pattern is durable, reusable, and waterproof; therefore, it is suitable for wet grinding. The Mylar® pattern is cut into pattern pieces prior to lamp construction, and each pattern piece is numbered and lettered. Appropriate pieces have arrows indicating the direction of glass streaks and color shading when cutting glass. Odyssey also produces a complete line of exact Tiffany reproduction hardware and accessories needed to finish your lamp in a professional manner. Besides rims, rings, jewels, filigree, and bronze crowns, precise reproduction lamp bases are also available.

(2) The Rainbow System: (Studio Design, Inc.)

This method of lamp shade construction utilizes a strong plastic form that is re-usable. Although some of the patterns are imprinted on sectional forms, these forms are connected prior to lamp construction to provide a 360° mold. The design pattern is incised on the inside of the form, and the lamp is constructed on the *inside* of the mold. Thus, the surface of the lamp will be completely even with variation in glass thickness projecting to the inside of the lamp. This is the only system in which construction is on the inside of the form. Each Rainbow kit also includes a paper pattern, instructions, and suggested square footage of glass needed. Rainbow offers a limited selection of accessories (molded fruit and dragon fly, jewels, and filigree) and 6 lamp base kits. The lamp bases are fabricated from glass, utilizing the same Rainbow system. There is a wiring kit and a metal base for completion of the lamp bases.

(3) The Whittemore Durgin System:

A component approach is utilized with forms, patterns, and an instruction book sold separately. There are currently five lamp molds available with over 170 patterns offered for use with these forms. The molds are complete 360° forms constructed of styrene and can be used repeatedly. Twenty-seven of the patterns are Tiffany-style reproductions, and the rest are in Art Nouveau and modern styles. It is necessary to make two to three copies of the supplied paper pattern. One of these copies is cut to provide pattern pieces, one is cut with gussets (indicated on the pattern) and applied to the lamp mold, and the other pattern is used for reference. The Whittemore Durgin mail order catalog also offers glass packages with a sufficient quantity of glass to complete each lamp. Although glass color is consistent, the manufacturer of the glass is at the discretion of Whittemore Durgin. The catalog offers zinc alloy bases and an extensive selection of lamp hardware, accessories and electrical fittings.

(4) The Worden System:

Over 160 designs are currently offered, and most of these are constructed on sectional forms. Worden has recently added five different full 360° molds to their line as well. When lamps are constructed using a sectional form, each section of the lamp is completed and soldered individually; then, the sections are joined together to complete a 360° shape. A Worden kit contains a mold (either sectional or complete), a paper pattern, an instruction manual, and Magic Strip sheets. The forms are plain, and the Magic Strip sheets are cut into horizontal strips that are applied to the mold using glue, double stick tape or pins. Worden offers an extensive line of lamp accessories, including filigree, glass jewels, glass apples and pears, cast brass heat caps, cast brass spider legs, and brass vase caps. An embossed brass band is available for use with a glass crown.

There are numerous similarities as well as differences in the offerings of these four companies. Besides the recommendation of choosing a fairly simple lamp with 400—600 pieces and avoiding extensive gridwork for your first project, the most important recommendation is to choose a lamp shade with a style and design that is compatible with your taste. Visiting museums and stores with examples or exhibits of stained glass lamps is helpful. Also, bookstores and public libraries may be a valuable resource for pictures and descriptions of stained glass lamps and their use as art objects. You will be spending many hours on this project, and it is essential for you to choose a lamp which you will enjoy.

c. Inspection of Kit and Preparation of Pattern and Mold

(1) General Instructions:

The first task is to inspect your kit and make certain that all components are present, free of damage, and the correct design. Read the instructional manual to achieve an overall perspective of the steps involved in your particular system. It is useful to have three or four pattern copies; one for the form, one to cut out and use as a glass pattern, one to use for reference, and one to color. The patterns can be copied using carbon paper, tracing the pattern on

Mylar®, pattern board, or heavy paper. If using a commercial copier, make certain that the copy is identical to the original by holding it up to a light source. Even minor distortions will result in problems when fitting glass.

It is a good idea to color one of your paper patterns with colored pencils so when cutting, you can quickly identify what all the shapes represent. Before doing this however, take some time to study the pattern and decide how all of the shapes would look in life. Note where one leaf overlaps another; where a flower appears to be viewed from an angle instead of straight on; or where a long stem is bisected by an overlapping leaf. Keep in mind that the letter identifications shown on your pattern are not an absolute rule. They are only one solution to the resolution of shapes. The shape or grouping of most pieces make it obvious what they are supposed to represent—a flower, leaf, etc. Others, however, are more ambiguous. It is difficult to tell what they are supposed to be. One piece might be seen as a flower or a leaf or background, depending on how you look at it. Even original Tiffany lamps are often inconsistent in this way. A certain pattern piece was often colored as a flower on one repeat, as a leaf on the second, and as background on the third! There are no firm rules. You are the artist. The way you see it is the correct way. The important thing is to arrive at a mental picture of what you are trying to represent and use the qualities of the glass to make that picture come alive in your lamp.

Keep this in mind when coloring your pattern: shade your flowers the way you want to shade the glass. Make that leaf a little darker where it tucks under the one in front of it. Note that two pieces are parts of the same stem, and color them the same. On your pattern, indicate that a certain piece could either be a flower or a leaf by crosshatching it green in one direction and red in the other. A little time spent formulating a plan of attack in the beginning can really make a difference in your finished lamp.

One of your patterns will need to be cut out to provide a glass cutting pattern. Read the instructions carefully about this process for your particular kit.

If you are unsure about how much lead allowance to give yourself, do a test by photo-copying a section of your pattern, cutting out about a dozen adjacent pattern pieces, and cutting along the edges of the black line. Copy these in glass and see how they fit on the mold. (You should have less than ¹⁄₃₂″ average gap between pieces with ¹⁄₆₄″ being ideal.) Then make the adjustments needed when you cut out your cutting pattern. Double-cutting pattern shears are not recommended on patterns with small intricate curves as they tend to bind up, leaving jagged edges. Use a sharp pair of good quality utility scissors, along with some patience.

As the pattern pieces are cut out, organize them by making up a set of envelopes, one for each category (flower, leaf, etc.) and sort all the pattern pieces into the proper envelopes. Then as you cut, take only the pieces out of the envelope representing the type of glass or area you are cutting and lay them out on the reference sheet. If the pattern is a large one, say over 400 pieces, you may want to subdivide your pattern into smaller areas. Divide your pattern into two or more separate sections by drawing a heavy black line on your reference pattern at the boundary between sections, and number each section. Then subdivide all your envelopes of pattern pieces by section, labeling them 'leaves, Section 2,' 'flowers, Section 1,' etc. This will significantly cut down on the time you spend finding pattern pieces.

(2) Preparation of Mold:

After receiving your mold you will need to prepare it before it is ready to use. Each system is different and each company will be considered separately.

(a) Odyssey: If you plan to use a lamp jig to support your mold, you will need to do some preliminary modifications in order to mount the mold at the aperture as this can produce undue stress on the mold, particularly when inclined on its side during soldering operations.

Mount it by means of a wooden disc installed in the bottom of the mold. Use ½″ to ¾″ plywood to cut a disc that will just clear the inside of the mold. Temporarily secure the disc by placing the mold over it on a level surface and drilling three or four small holes through the fiberglass into the wooden disc. Insert nails into each of these holes, so that when the mold is turned upside down the plywood disc will remain in position. The disc should be glued to the mold rather than being secured by screws or nails as these will force the mold out of round if there is any gap between the two. We recommend using fiberglass resin as a glue because it sets up quickly and will provide a permanent bond to the fiberglass mold.

Before gluing, wrap a piece of masking tape around the entire bottom edge of the mold so that most of the width of the tape hangs out over the edge. This will act as a dam to prevent resin from dripping onto the outside of the mold and getting into the engraved lines. Due to the thinness of the liquid resin, it will take several applications to fill the gap between the plywood and the mold. In places where there

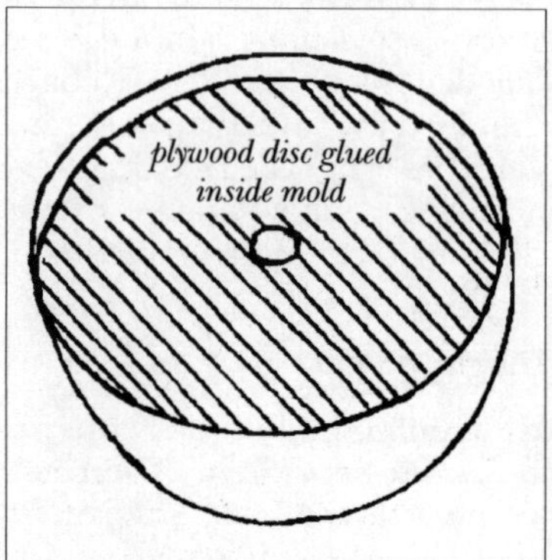

Figure 21.7: Lamp jig

plywood disc glued inside mold

are wide gaps, the first application will form only a film across the gap. Do not keep pouring resin into the gap if it appears to be going right on through. Wait for the resin to set up and apply another coat. If the gap is really large, you may want to stuff some strips of cloth into it to provide a bridge. In any event, the final coat should fill the gap all the way around. When this final coat has set-up, remove the nails and sand off any excess resin. (see *Figure 21.7*)) A pipe flange can then be screwed into the center of the wooden plate and this in turn used to adapt to your lamp stand.

The lines engraved into the mold are permanent, but they are difficult to see and need to be filled with colored tile grout to bring them out. A good grout mixture can be made from the following:

Grout
3 tsp. powered tile grout (without sand)
½ tsp. powdered black tile grout pigment
½ tsp. white glue (Elmer's®, Wilhold®, etc.
3 tsp. water (approximately)

Use only tile grout pigment as other pigments may tend to smear and not clean up as well. You will want the above mixture to have the consistency of pea soup, so start by mixing only two teaspoons of water, and then add more until the consistency is correct. Smear the grout over the entire surface of the mold with your fingers, taking care to see that you work it into all the engraved lines. Then use dry paper towels or rags to clean off the excess. Don't expect to get it all off in one wiping. Go over the entire mold with one set of towels and again with a clean set. This should remove the vast majority of it, leaving only a thin gray film over the entire mold. If you want your mold white again, wait an hour or so until the grout begins to set up and go over it again with a rag only slightly damp. If the rag is too wet, it will begin to drag grout out of the grooves. After drying, the grayness can be completely removed with sandpaper if desired. Use 280 to 400 grit only as anything coarser will unduly scratch the mold. After grouting, give the mold at least a day to dry out before coating it with wax.

(b) Rainbow: This mold requires minimal preparation. It is necessary to punch out the imprinted seam holes with a hammer and nail or drill. The sections of the mold are then joined using the provided screws. If needed, additional holes can be drilled through the seams and fastened, using nuts and bolts to provide a closer fit. Make certain that the seams are even and the bottom is level. Attach the form to a lamp leveling device such as Worden's Lampleveler® or place the form in a bucket, dishpan, or carton. (See *Figure 21.8.a and Figure 21.8.b*)

(c) Whittemore-Durgin: This form is plain and must be covered with a paper pattern. It is suggested that the most legible pattern copy be used for this purpose. The pattern is cut out including the gussets indicated by dotted lines. After the pattern is cut out, it is positioned on the form and the meeting points are taped using cellophane tape. Do not attach the pattern to the form with tape as it should be free enough to be lifted off. Finally the lamp is secured to the top circular portion of the lamp using masking tape. Try not to obscure much of the pattern. This securing will prevent the paper pattern from sliding down the form as the glass is placed on the mold.

Figure 21.8.a: Joining mold sections

Figure 21.8.b:
Lamp leveling device

(d) H. L. Worden: Both the sectional and complete forms are blank. There are parallel ridges around the mold similar to the latitudinal lines on a globe. The Magic strips™ are cut out along the inside edge of the dotted lines. Each of the strips is coded with a number and letter corresponding to a number and letter on the form. The strips are attached to the mold using pins, sticky tape, or a thin coat of glue (G. E. Silicone #361 works well) between the ridges. For sectional forms side boards are recommended. These prevent the glass sections from being slightly larger than appropriate. Side boards are supplied with your sectional kit and are placed along each edge of the form using pins and/or glue (either GE #361 silicone or Elmer's® white glue). (See *Figure 21.9*)

d. Choosing Glass

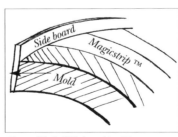

Figure 21.9: Side board position

Without a doubt, the single most important factor determining how your finished lamp shade will look is your choice of glass. It is important to avoid the use of monochromatic, flat-appearing glass. The most careful technical workmanship will not compensate for inferior glass selection. On the other hand, a lamp shade exhibiting only mediocre workmanship will be breathtaking if the glass is of good quality and skillfully used.

The glass used in Tiffany lamps is usually opalescent, to at least some degree. Opalescent glass is differentiated from what is known as cathedral glass by the presence of a chemical agent in the glass that scatters light. This characteristic is significant to the lamp maker because he is working around a single light source rather than a diffused light source (such as sky). A lamp shade made of cathedral glass will only light up in the area directly in front of the light bulb. The rest of the shade will appear much darker or even black. The diffusing characteristic of opalescent glass makes the whole lamp shade light up, no matter from where it is viewed. In short, cathedral glass is rarely used in lamp shades except for specialized effects. Opalescent glass is available in a wide variety of opacities, colors, and textures.

The lamp maker is an artist whose palette is colored glass. The richer and more interesting the palette, the better the lamp will be. Choose your glass for the depth and variety it contains as well as its color. Of course, the choice of glass and color is a highly subjective matter. The following suggestions may be helpful, particularly when reproducing Tiffany lamps. These ideas are intended as a guide, however, rather than a hindrance, and the daring may throw convention to the wind to produce a work of unique, individual appearance.

Think in terms of what you are trying to represent when choosing glass for your lamp shade. In general, solid objects look best in glass with at least moderate opacity to give the impression that they are solid. Background areas lend themselves to a more transparent glass, often incorporating texture and/or fractures to help scatter the light. Backgrounds also usually look best when done in a cool color (the blue, green, purple range) that is more muted than the foliage in front of them. This does not apply to geometric backgrounds (such as the pansy, black-eyed susan, poinsettia etc.), which may be fairly opaque and often look good in warmer tones (amber for example).

The amount of glass required to complete any particular lamp shade depends on more than just how big it is. If your color is monochromatic and the cuts fairly simple, three times the surface area of the shade should be adequate. Factors such as cutting skill, intricate shapes, color shading and glass 'cut-ability' all increase the amount of glass that will be necessary. Estimating your requirement becomes more difficult the more you demand from your work. Sometimes 15 to 20 times the area is not excessive! In any event, buy all you need before you start, because there's nothing more frustrating than running out of a particular glass only to discover that your supplier has run out too!

Sometimes, it is overwhelming to try to select all of the glass for your lamp at one time. It may be easier to divide your lamp pattern into elements of themes i.e., flowers, leaves, stems, background. Select glass for one element and cut it out. After you have completed cutting out that one element, 'wax-up' (see next lesson), return to the glass supplier and select another element, comparing the

new glass to your 'waxed-up' model. Continue this process until all the glass is selected. If you decide to follow this method, remember to make careful notes about the glass you have used, so it can be replicated in each repeat.

To avoid a paint-by-number appearance, it is necessary to blend colors within elements. For example, if your lamp contains pink flowers, it is very helpful to have some of your leaves contain pink. This will soften the harsh delineation imposed by lead lines. Also, including some pink areas in the background glass will further soften and blend the design elements so that there will be a more natural appearance. (See *Figure 21.7*)

The use of texture within the design elements will add highlights and interest. A few pieces of ripple included in a flower, for example, will greatly enhance the three-dimensional look. Textured glass is often used in borders; the ripple usually is turned to the inside of the lamp, but there are no strict rules about this.

e. Cutting Glass

Although it is very difficult to decide to cut a particular piece so that it will have the best color and shading, the actual cutting is pretty straight-forward. The choice of a glass cutter and the decision of whether to cut against the pattern or mark around it with a felt pen are matters of personal preference and experience.

If you have access to a light table, it can be useful in selecting the particular part of a sheet of glass to use, as well as seeing how all the glass pieces you have cut work together. The fitting process should be started only after all the glass for your lamp is cut. The light table should be illuminated by light bulbs rather than fluorescent tubes, as incandescent light will be your ultimate light source. Incandescent light is much redder than either fluorescent light or daylight, and glass will appear differently in each. The wattage necessary to properly illuminate glass on a light table is far greater than the wattage adequate to illuminate the lampshade when it's finished. One hundred watts per square foot of light table surface is a good rule of thumb to follow. The glass covering the table should be clear, because frosted glass will change the apparent opacity of your glass, as well as obscure some of the subtler effects.

After cutting, it is often helpful to 'wax-up' your lamp pieces on a sheet of safety plate glass to be able to visualize the completed appearance of the lamp prior to fitting the pieces on the mold. The 'wax-up' also provides an excellent way to keep track of all the pieces. The plate glass should be large enough to accommodate at least one section; the edges can be covered with masking tape or heat polished to prevent accidental cuts. Caution should be exercised regarding storage of your 'waxed-up' model in a warm place (for example a sunlit window). The wax may melt and the pieces fall off. Tacky Wax (Odyssey) is excellent for 'waxing-up' and does not impart color to the glass pieces while viewing. It is easy to transfer the pieces from the plate glass to the form, using a small palette knife to facilitate lifting the waxed pieces from the plate glass.

Special Note. Remember when cutting glass for a Rainbow System lamp that you will be working on the *inside* of the mold. Glass pieces will be placed front side down in the form.

f. Fitting:

This is an exciting process when the glass pieces are transferred to the mold for a final fitting prior to foiling.

The glass pieces should fit fairly snugly together on the mold, but should not have to be crammed into place. Remember that you need a little room to accommodate the foil, so there should be some play between pieces. ½₂" to ¹⁄₆₄" is ideal, with ¹⁄₁₆" being the maximum allowable gap. If the gap is larger than this in some places, move pieces slightly to distribute the gap over a wide area. Use your grinder and grozing pliers to trim glass only where it prevents pieces from fitting correctly on the mold. Your patterns and mold lines are only guides to help you. In the end, how your lamp fits on, or in, the mold is what really matters.

On the other hand, don't get so sloppy that you lose the sense of what you are trying to represent. Border rows and geometric backgrounds should be kept straight and regular. Stem and leaf lines should not become jagged or wobbly when they aren't supposed to look that way. Most flower petals have rounded contours and should not be left with angular corners in inappropriate places, even though they might fit okay on the mold. In general, when trimming glass to go on the mold, remember the sense of what you are trying to represent and how it's going to appear with lead lines around it. Specific differences in fitting for the four systems are discussed separately as follows.

(1) Odyssey: The pieces of glass are held on the mold by a thin coating of Tacky Wax brushed hot onto the mold. The quantity of wax required to cover the mold varies from less than ⅛ lb. for a 16" dome to ½ lb. for a 28" dome. Melt more wax than you will need as the extra is easily saved for your next project; however, save at least one stick (2 oz.) from the melt for other uses that will be described later.

Melt the wax in a double boiler or tin can and continue heating it until it reaches a temperature of about 240°F. You can use a candy thermometer the first few times to get the feel of it. (Don't worry, the wax will not poison your next batch of fudge as it is no more toxic than paraffin.) **But Use Caution! This wax is flammable like paraffin and can burst into flame if heated over 400°F.** The wax is then brushed onto the mold with a bristle paint brush, using long, even strokes. One thin coat is all that is necessary. If the wax is not hot enough, the coating will be too thick or 'cakey' when applied. If too hot, the wax will curl the bristles of your brush. Plastic or nylon bristles

can't be used as they cannot take the heat. Use only natural bristle brushes.

After being waxed, the mold should be covered with a plastic garbage bag when not being used to prevent it from collecting grease and dust out of the air. It will not lose its tackiness with time.

Begin fitting the glass pieces onto your waxed mold, starting from the top down. Set your Odyssey ring or vase cap in the recess at the top of the mold and use it to position your upper row of glass. Do not rely on the recessed lip itself to position the glass, as it is a little larger than the actual ring. If using a vase cap, you will need to prop it up to the level of the glass by placing 3 or 4 balls of Tacky Wax underneath to hold it in place. The glass should adhere to the waxed mold with gentle pressing. If it won't stick, the glass is probably a little greasy and needs to be cleaned. Often a slight twisting motion will help 'set' the glass pieces. Large glass pieces (such as dragonfly wings or hydrangea blossoms) can be helped to stay in place by the addition of 2 or 3 balls of Tacky Wax underneath near their edges.

(2) Rainbow: It may be helpful to place a vase cap in the bottom of the mold (top of shade) to keep a perfect circle on the top of the shade. The pieces are placed in the form from the bottom of the mold to the top, working in a circle rather than by sections. When you have put as many pieces as possible in the mold without their falling, stop and foil the pieces. Replace the pieces and lightly tack solder into place. You many need to adjust pieces later, so the less solder the better at this stage. Continue to add rows of pieces, make necessary adjustments, foil, replace, and tack solder until the last piece is in place.

(3) Whittemore-Durgin: This manufacturer recommends that after the glass is cut, six to 12 pieces are foiled and placed on the form, using double faced masking tape or by using ordinary masking tape that is folded over so it is sticky on two sides. The recommended size for the pieces of tape is ¼ x ¼". The tape is placed in the center of each piece of glass; when the glass is pressed against the paper pattern it will adhere. After the first six to twelve pieces are applied to the paper and the fit is checked, the pieces are tack soldered. Check the fit for each additional piece, foil, stick to the form with the tape, and tack solder in place.

As the pieces are added, there is an increase in weight applied to the pattern covering the form. If some of the pieces are held away from the form due to wrinkling of the paper pattern, it is important to push them snug to the form prior to tacking. When applying pieces of glass to the upper and lower edges, use masking tape to tape them directly to the exposed edges of the form providing additional strength and stability while soldering. This process is continued until all the pieces are tacked into place.

(4) Worden: These forms are made of styrofoam, and it is recommended that glass pieces be held in place using pins (glass headed, plastic headed, or common pins 1 to 1¼"). Place all the pieces on the form to insure fit and final adjustment prior to foiling.

g. Foiling:

Foil your lamp by removing the glass pieces one at a time, foiling them, and replacing them on the mold. A sturdy, pointed tool or palette knife thin enough to fit between the glass pieces is useful to help in prying them loose.

Choose a width of foil that will give you between ⅟₆₄" and ⅟₃₂" overlap on both the front and back surfaces of the glass. This is all that is necessary to hold the glass piece securely in place and provide adequate structural strength for the lamp. The amount of overlap is determined by the gap between glass pieces and the size of the pieces. For aesthetic reasons the resultant lead line should range from ⅟₃₂" to ⅛" in width, with slightly broader lead lines acceptable for lamps with very large pieces (such as Hydrangea) and narrower lead lines permissible for small piece designs (such as the Wisteria and Laburnum). If your cutting has resulted in wide gaps between pieces, you should foil with a minimum of overlap to avoid ending up with very wide lead lines. Unless you are trying to create a special effect or design element, wide lead lines do not look good. Because foil comes in limited widths, it may be necessary at times to trim the edges of a length of foil using an X-acto® knife and straight edge or a pair of scissors.

(l) Foiling Tips:

* Begin and end your foil strip on the sharpest corner of the glass piece. No overlap is necessary. Don't start foiling on the center of a smooth edge because you will create a jagged edge in the lead line if your foil doesn't line up perfectly.

* Use a smooth surfaced metal tool (such as a burnisher or ice pick) to press the foil down flat on both the front and back surfaces of the glass. Foil not pressed down flat will result in rough lead lines as well as providing a place for residual wax and flux to accumulate, which may later interfere with your patina. Be sure the tool you use for this is smooth so it doesn't tear the foil.

* For glass pieces along the rim or aperture edge, do not start the foil along the exposed edge (even at the corner). The exposed end may become loose and separate later during the soldering or shade removal operations.

* Foiling glass pieces for irregular thicknesses (such as ripple or drapery) presents special problems. Most ripple glass can be foiled with a standard foil width that overlaps a little too much in the valleys and doesn't quite make it over the ridges. Occasional tearing on the overlap is to be expected and is acceptable. When the glass is extremely variable in thickness (such as ½" drapery!) use a foil width

appropriate for the thinner areas, and augment it with short strips to get overlap in thick areas.

In recent years there has been a renewed interest in cutting foil strips from waxed sheet copper. This was the method utilized before copper foil strips became commercially available. The major advantage for commercially available strips is the convenience of a good product with minimal clean up problems. Waxed foil is slightly more malleable, will stand-up to the chemicals used for copper plating, (the acrylic glue used with commercial foil may seep out underneath the lead lines when exposed to plating chemicals) and there is greater control over foil width. The disadvantage to using waxed foil is that there will be a thin film of wax on the glass after soldering that will need to be cleaned off the lamp using petroleum solvents.

2) Method for Waxing Foil:

TOOLS AND MATERIALS:
Lectro-stik® waxer
Sheet copper foil
Tacky Wax®
Waxed paper
X-acto® knife (blades)
Metal straight edge and or T-Square

(The above materials are available from Odyssey.)

The waxer needs to be loaded with small pieces of wax and plugged into an electrical outlet for about 30 minutes prior to using. A one to two foot length of 12" sheet copper is cut and taped securely to a table (covering table with newspaper will help with cleanup). The waxer is then rolled over the foil in horizontal strips, making one pass for each strip. After the foil is covered with a thin layer of wax the process may be repeated using vertical strips. Now lay waxed paper down on the waxed surface of the foil to protect the surface from lint and dirt. When waxing process is completed, merely unplug waxer, allow to cool and store till the next time (no clean up needed).

When ready to cut the foil, adhere it to a flat surface copper side up. You will be cutting through the copper and waxed paper. Use a new X-acto® blade for each one-two square feet of foil. Be sure to check blades for burrs that will tear rather than cut. Using a metal straight edge or T-square, cut the foil in strips of desired width.

This process is probably easier that it sounds. You can wax several sheets of foil at one time, store them in a flat container protected from light and heat, and cut into strips as needed. Air oxidizes copper, however, so it should be used within one to two months.

h. Soldering:

The soldering step is where all those pieces you cut, fit, and foiled are finally joined together into a lampshade. Once the lamp is soldered together, it is difficult to replace pieces or make changes, so before starting, check to see that everything is exactly where you want it to be on the mold.

Your soldering work area should be well lit and well ventilated. If there is little air movement in the room, use a fan to keep the soldering fumes away from your face as an absolute minimum. All fumes should be vented to the outside, if at all possible.(See Chapter 25, *Health and Safety*) You will need to position your lamp at many different angles, so some means of keeping it stable is a necessity. A lamp leveling device is perfect for this, but a few appropriately sized cardboard boxes will work satisfactorily.

Look for the following:

* *Large gaps between pieces.* Shove adjacent pieces around to spread out the gap.

* *Disturbed foil.* The foil may have become unstuck or been crammed out of place accidently while foiling. Fix it now.

* *Straight geometric lines.* Be especially careful that border rows and gridwork areas are aligned so as to produce straight regular lead lines. Trim foil edges if necessary to make the bead width consistent along its entire length. Nothing looks worse than lead lines that are wobbly or uneven when they should be straight.

(1) Sequence of Procedures:

The soldering of your shade should be done in a definite sequence with variation as per lamp construction system used

(a)Odyssey:

   i. Tin the outside of the shade.
   ii. Release the shade from the mold.
   iii. Install the ring and rim where applicable.
   iv. Tin and bead the inside of the shade.
   v. Bead the outside of the shade.

(b) Rainbow:

   i. Tin and bead (optional) the inside of the tacked shade.
   ii. Release the shade from the mold.
   iii. Tin and bead the outside of the shade.
   iv. Apply 10-12 gauge copper wire to top and bottom edges then bead solder.

(c) Whittemore-Durgin:

   i. Tin the outside of the shade.
   ii. Release the shade from the mold.
   iii. Tin and bead the inside of the shade.
   iv. Bead the outside of the shade.
   v. Apply 10-12 gauge copper wire to top and bottom edges and bead over the wire.

(d) Worden Full Form:

   i. Tack solder and remove pins (except the bottom row).
   ii. Tin the outside of the shade.
   iii. Release the shade from the form.
   iv. Install 10-12 gauge wire at top and bottom edges.
   v. Tin and bead inside of shade.
   vi. Bead outside of shade.

(e) Worden Sectional Form:

   i. Tack solder and remove pins (except the bottom row).
   ii. Tin the outside of the shade.
   iii. Remove from form, clean, and store 'carefully' until all sections are completed.
   iv. Join sections using adjustable solder loops.
   v. Install 10-12 gauge copper wire at top and bottom edge.
   vi. Tin and bead solder the inside of the shade.
   vii. Bead the outside of the shade.

Ed. Note—Some long-time lamp builders recommend: that if tack soldering first __instead__ of tinning, the Tacky Wax does not melt all over the inside of the lamp, necessitating extensive wax removal. Take a single edge razor blade and scrape as much wax as possible off the shade, then place shade back on mold to tin.

(2) Tinning

Before beginning this step, be sure you will have time to work through to the inside soldering step within a day or two. The flux you are applying is corrosive to the copper foil in your lamp and will eventually produce a green encrustation that is difficult to solder through. Even though you are working on the outside of the lamp, some of the melted flux will get through to the inside. The inside must be tinned before it corrodes, so *don't even start soldering if you are going to have to leave the lamp untinned on the inside for any length of time.*

Some of the lamp forms tuck in or curve at the bottom (such as 16" cone 22" dragonfly 18" and 22" turbans). Odyssey patterns are constructed on 360° molds it is not possible to remove these tucked shades without following a special procedure. Please see the special section on soldering tucked shades.

Begin by brushing the entire outside of the shade with paste flux. A paste flux is recommended because it does not contain water, which will cause sputtering and bubbles. Don't be skimpy with the flux; too much is better than too little, and you can always wipe the excess off later. Next, tin the entire outside with solder, using the largest soldering iron you have. You want the solder to penetrate all the way through to the inside of the shade, so the more heat the better. We recommend a 250 watt iron if you have one and also the muscles to hold it!! Penetration of the solder is important to provide strength to the shade, and also to prevent air pockets from being created inside the lead lines. The air pockets will cause sputtering and bubbles when you solder the inside of the shade due to the water and/or oils trapped in them. Water based fluxes are especially prone to cause sputtering and for this reason should be avoided. Don't try to bead the outside of the shade at this step; it is better left until later. With Rainbow, you can tin and bead the inside of the shade before removing it from the form.

If your shade has an irregular lower border, install the rim wire around the lower edge before the shade is removed from the form (not applicable with a sectional form). Twelve gauge copper wire is best for this purpose although higher gauges (thinner wire) are acceptable. First, remove any solder drips protruding from the edge of the shade, so the wire will fit flush against the edge. Begin the wire at the highest point in the rim, attaching it at the joint with solder. Use a pair of needle nose pliers to help bend the wire around intricate curves. Keep it as flush as possible against the edge, but do not cut the wire at angles. A tight curve around the angle is better than cutting the wire, which will weaken the integrity of the rim. Connect it only at the solder joints until the entire rim is in place. Then go back and tin the rim to the edge foil again without beading.

(3) Release From Mold:

Release of the shade from the form is quite simple in all situations except where Tacky Wax has been used. Worden, Rainbow and Whittemore-Durgin (after cutting tape attaching glass to the form) simply lift off. The instructions for removing an Odyssey lamp follows:

(a) Odyssey: To release the shade from the form. it must be heated to 150°F. in order to melt the wax. Three methods are recommended:

    i. Oven: If the shade is small enough, set it in a cold oven with aluminum foil or a cookie sheet underneath to catch the melted wax. Set the thermostat to 200° F. and leave it in for 15–20 minutes or until the glass becomes hot to the touch.

    ii Light Bulb: Set a 100 watt light bulb (on large shades, use more light bulbs for a longer amount of time) mounted on a porcelain base inside the fiberglass mold for 20–30 minutes.

    iii. Hair Dryer: Use a hair dryer (at least 1000 watt) set on its highest setting about 4″ from the glass. Move it continuously and evenly about the shade being careful not to point it at one spot for too long.

Glass can crack from heat shock, so patience is necessary. Don't be surprised if it takes one-half hour on a large shade to get it warm enough to remove. The wax does not have to be dripping out the bottom for it to be hot enough. The glass, though, should be quite warm to the touch all over. When the lamp is hot enough to remove, gentle pulling should release it. If you have to use a lot of pressure, the shade is not warm enough yet. It's easier if you get some help to do this; one person to hold the form down in the center and the other to lift from the rim on both sides.

Mental Health Warning: If you have been trying for over an hour to release your shade off the mold, and it just won't come, do not become impatient or violent. You are in an emotional state that could cause serious damage to your lampshade. It's time to take a mental health break and reconsider this operation. Have a cup of herbal tea or eat some chocolate cake and then re-read these instructions slowly. If they still don't provide the answer you are looking for, please call the Hotline (1-800-228-2613).

As soon as the shade is off the mold, check the rim and ring at the exposed edges to see that the foil has not pulled away from the glass. It should be pressed back up against the glass before the wax is solidified, or you will have to replace foil.

Next wipe the wax off the mold using paper towels. Again, this is much easier to do while the wax is still soft.

Do not attempt to clean the wax off the inside of the shade at this point.

(4) Joining Glass Sections

Many of the Worden lamps are constructed on sectional forms. After each section is tinned, it is necessary to join them to create a completed lamp. It is critical for the sections to be lined up carefully with particular emphasis on keeping the bottom level. Probably the best method for the beginner is the *Two Sectional Form* method described on page 10 of the *Wordensystem™ Instructional Manual*, 1990. Another method is described on pages four and five of this same manual. This method utilizes loops of solder applied between sections to allow adjustments prior to the final soldering of the sections together. Both methods are really quite simple once you understand. However, if you are frustrated after studying the manual, there is a technical assistance hotline (800) 541-1103. Also, don't hesitate to ask a friend to hold the sections while you tack solder them together.

(5) Finishing Top and Bottom Edges

(a) Install the Brass Ring and Rim.

If using a brass ring to finish the top edge of your lamp, it should be applied after the first tinning step is completed and the lamp is removed from the mold. A brass rim can be applied to the lower border at this time as well. Unless you are planning to have your lamp electroplated, you will need to tin the ring and rim prior to installation. Place objects to be trimmed on a heat-proof surface, apply flux generously and apply solder using a soldering iron or small propane torch. Cover brass with a thin smooth coat of solder.

The brass rim and ring will provide strength. It will help keep the shape true and protect the edges during the final soldering operations.

Install the ring first. Remove any solder drips from the edge of the rim, so the shade will sit flat on a table. Solder the ring to the shade in three places, at the joints approximately 120° apart. With two, three and four inch rings, the upper edge of the ring should protrude slightly above the outside contour of the lamp, with the majority of ring depth left on the inside of the shade.

With five and six inch rings, the glass should rest against the lower side of the bead around the ring with the long flange of the ring facing downward. The foil on the outside aperture edge should be widened so that it's edge is directly below the edge of ring bead. (See *Figure 21.10*)

Before completely soldering the ring into the shade, it must be leveled. You will need a straight edge longer than the diameter of the shade and a ruler taller than the shade. Place the straight edge across the top of the ring and measure both ends of it with your ruler from the table up. Note where it is high or low. Rotate the straight edge 90° and repeat your measurements. If the difference between measurements is less than ⅟₁₆″ across the shade, you can assume the ring is level in that direction. If the difference is greater than ⅟₁₆″. loosen the appropriate solder joint (one

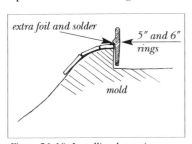

Figure 21.10: Installing brass ring

at time!), raise or lower the ring, and re-attach. Repeat your measurements, and re-adjust until the difference is less than ⅟₁₆ ″ in all directions. Then double check yourself by taking another set of measurements at 45° from your last set. If you're satisfied that the ring is level, solder it into the shade all the way around, both outside and inside.

(b) Install copper wire on top and bottom edges.

Instead of the brass rim and ring, a copper wire can be applied to the top and bottom edges. Twelve gauge wire is best for this purpose but thinner wire (higher gauges) are acceptable. The new flexible braided copper wire may also be used. Bend a ring of wire slightly larger than the diameter of the upper opening. It is often easiest to start soldering in the middle of the ring and work toward the ends. After tacking in two or three places trim the ends with nippers to fit exactly. The wire ring should be flush with the glass edges. Fill in the gaps and completely cover with solder.

Reinforce a regular bottom edge in the same manner as the top. (For applying wire to irregular bottom edge please, see section on tinning). (See *Figure 21.11*)

(c) Install a vase cap:

If you are using a vase cap instead of a ring in the top of your lamp, leveling measurements are unnecessary. It will automatically level itself because the shade will be supported only in the center. Tack it in three places and check to see that the outside contour of the vase cap flows into the outside contour of the shade all the way around. Readjust until it does, then solder the vase cap into the shade. (See *Figure 21.12*)

Next install the rim. First check it to be sure it is level, circular and within an inch of the circumference of the shade. Hand bending will usually take care of any minor irregularities. Place one end of the rim between joints and solder it to the edge of the shade at a joint about 2″

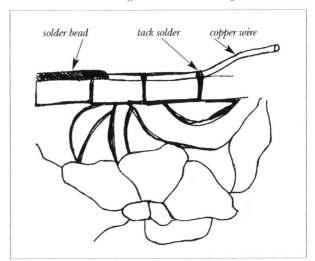

Figure 21.11: Reinforcing top/bottom edges

from the end. Move down another 4″ to 6″ and attach it at another joint. Try not to get solder on top of the rim, (assuming the shade is now upside down). Repeat this spacing all the way around the shade until you can tell where the end of the rim should be trimmed off to meet flush with the other end. Use a hacksaw to cut off the excess rim wire. Attach the rim to itself (but not to the foil below), and check to see that a slight angle is not created at the joint. Next place the shade right side up on a level surface and see where the rim raises up off the table. In the high areas, melt the solder attachment with your soldering iron, push the rim down with a screwdriver until it touches the table, and re-attach the joint. Repeat this process until the entire rim is flush against the table. This will insure that your rim will be level. Now you can completely solder it onto the shade, both inside and out.

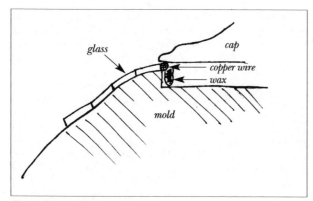

Figure 21.12: Installing a vase cap

(6) Finish Soldering

After the rim and ring are installed, you can go ahead and complete the soldering of the shade. We recommend that you tin and bead the inside before beading the outside. Beading often produces solder drips on the other side of the shade which are easy to miss. If the outside is beaded last, these drips will be hidden where no one is likely to spot them.

If Tacky Wax has been used the bulk of it left on the shade can be removed while tinning the inside. The wax will melt and form a pool which can be soaked up with Kleenex as you go along. The wax will not interfere with the flow of the solder onto the foil.

If the shade is larger than 22″ in diameter, reinforcement wires also need to be added to the inside for extra support. Twelve or fourteen gauge copper wire is best for this purpose. Use three to six wires (depending on the size), running all the way from the ring of the shade to the rim. About ½″ of wire is soldered up against the ring, then it follows the solder lines down to the lower rim of the shade. This is best done after the shade is tinned, but *before beading* because you want the wires to sit right up against the foil. (See *Figure 21.13*)

Beading deserves special attention because a lot of people seem to have trouble with it. Use a somewhat smaller iron, between 100 and 75 watts, as you need control rather than heat to bead. Provision must be made to hold the lamp steady at all angles, so that you can always be soldering on a horizontal surface. 'Third hand' jigs are available at your local stained glass supplier. Again flux all the solder lines to be beaded, even though there is a lot of flux left from the tinning operation. Keep the area that you are working on horizontal or the molten solder will flow toward the downhill side creating a bump or seam.

The trick to beading is using the *right* amount of solder with the *right* amount of heat for the *right* length of time. Too much solder will create a high bead that is hard to control. A good bead should be less than 180° curve, somewhere in the range of 120° to 140°. You want to

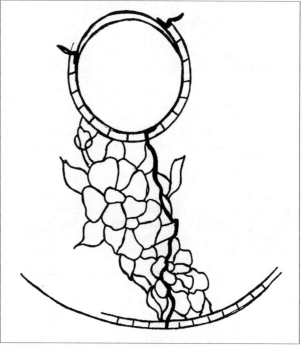

Figure 21.13: Additional reinforcement

apply enough heat to melt the solder from ⅛″ to ¼″ on each side of the iron tip, but not so much so that the solder sinks through to the other side. You also want to leave the iron on long enough to get the solder hot so it won't 'peak' when you pick it up, but not so long as to cause the solder to sink through. Often enough heat is provided by using only the corner of the iron tip on the edge of the bead. Work along the solder line, so the adjacent area is still hot and will blend with the area you are working on. This requires a good deal of patience at first, but with practice it will become easy. (See *Figure 21.14*)

When beading along the rim and ring edges, go all the way around at one time. The larger metal masses here create a 'heat sink' that is impossible to bead when cold. Don't be concerned if the bead is a little rough up against the brass rim or ring as these areas will be filed and sanded.

i. Special Techniques
(1) Soldering Tucked Shades

A tucked shade is one that curves more than 180° vertically across its surface. In other words, it is narrower at the rim, so the mold can't slip off. Shades in this category include the 16″ Cones, the 1 inch and 22″ Turbans and the 22″ Dragonfly. A tucked shade cannot be removed from a complete 360° mold if all the lead lines are tinned. To release, it must be left in two separate pieces much like the shells of a walnut. This is accomplished by leaving an unsoldered seam around the entire circumference at the

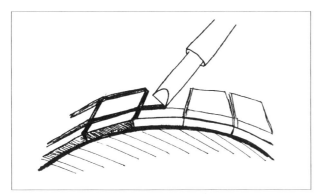

Figure 21.14: Beading the solder

widest point of the shade (at its widest point or the equator, so to speak) (See *Figure 21.15*) No part of this seam can be bridged by solder if the shade is to be removed from the mold. Before fluxing the outside of the shade, determine where this seam should be and mark the glass on both sides with a felt pen. The marked glass will help you to remember where the seam is while soldering. When the shade is ready to be released from the mold, you may need some tool such as a screwdriver or palette knife to help separate the two sections so you can get your fingers in between. As soon as the two sections are removed from the mold, press the foil back down along both sides of the seam and solder the two halves together. It is wise to first tack them only at eight or 10 joints around the shade to be sure the halves line up correctly before soldering them completely together.

Once the shade is in one piece, proceed with fitting the rim and ring and continue with soldering and finishing the lamp.

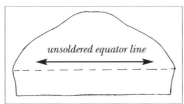

unsoldered equator line

Figure 21.15: Unsoldered line

(2) Filigree

Unless you are planning to have your lamp electroplated, you will need to tin the filigree so it will accept the patina. It is best to tin the filigree prior to installing on the lamp to avoid heat cracks in the underlying glass. Use a large soldering iron (100 watts) or a small one (60–100 watts). Coat filigree generously with paste flux. Place the wings on a flat, fire proof, clean surface and heat the metal sufficiently so the solder will flow and provide a thin smooth coat. Applying too much solder will cause it to fill in or bridge gaps in the filigree and all spaces in the filigree should be kept open.

Odyssey and Worden filigree is identical to that used on original Tiffany lamps. Rainbow and Whittemore-Durgin utilize the Worden filigree in their designs. In most cases, it is applied to the outside of the shade, the exception being the leaves on the 17″ and 20″ Poppy

cones where the leaf filigree may, as an option, be soldered to the inside. Because both the poppy and dragonfly filigrees are designed to fit more than one size shade, they sometimes must be trimmed on one side to fit correctly. Attach them only after the shade has been tinned on both sides. If there are solder lines underneath the filigree, they should be beaded before the filigree is applied and the filigree should not be attached to them.

During finishing of all filigreed lamps, the bead around the outside edge of all outside filigree should be filed down until it is flush with the surface of the filigree. Any file marks are removed with sandpaper.

The dragonflies present a special problem. The filigree for the underside wing must be trimmed, and the trimmed edge soldered to the side of the filigree on the overlapping wing. Because the overlapping wing stands out from the wing it covers, the underneath filigree will therefore bend away from the glass to completely cover the sloped wall.

On the Odyssey pattern for these shades, you will notice that there is typically a black space at the edge where the wings belonging to adjacent dragonflies meet. The reason for this space is a little complicated to explain, so please bear with me.

The dragonfly wings are long and flat, but rest against a curved surface, so they will naturally protrude above the surface of the mold at both ends. In preparing these shades for soldering, we push the wings in a little bit (but not all the way!) at the end touching the body and raise the body with balls of Tacky Wax so the whole area is flush. This raises the other end of the wing even further above the surface of the mold. Because the intersecting wings on adjacent dragonflies are not the same length (one is chopped off because the other one covers it), the full wing will protrude considerably above the chopped wing, sometimes as much as ¼″. This gap must be filled in with a thin wall of solder and beaded smooth on both sides. Our experience (and Tiffany's) has found that this wall is awkward to produce when it is vertical, so we have left a gap between the two wings on the pattern, giving the wall a distinct slope. This makes it easier to solder

The filigree on the full overlapping wing is attached to the solder line around its periphery except where it meets the body, and, at its end over the body which is attached to the other filigree. (See *Figure 21.16*)

(3) Wisteria Crown and Branch Set

At this time only Odyssey and Worden produce this hardware. Each will be discussed separately.

(a) Odyssey:

The Odyssey Crown and Branch set is an exact copy of the original Tiffany hardware, designed to be used on the Wisteria, Apple Blossom, Grape and Trumpet Vine. It consists of a 14″ machined bronze crown and 20 branch segments. You will need to do some clean up on the holes in the crown with a rat-tail file to make them smooth. The crown should also be tinned around the outside edge to make it easier to solder. To assemble the crown and branches, the crown is first positioned correctly on the form. Because it is slightly thinner than the branches, it will need to be propped up with several balls of Tacky Wax. The first branch is soldered securely to the crown in

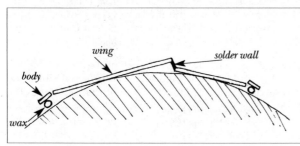

Figure 21.16: Attaching filigree

its correct position with a large soldering iron. A hammer is used to gently tap it down over the shoulder of the form until it is flat against the form. In most cases, you will need to bend the branches to one side or the other to get them aligned with the engraved lines on the mold. The branches are the correct length for the Wisteria, but with the Apple Blossom, some of them must be shortened with a pair of lead nips. Repeat this same process with the other 14 branches that butt up against the crown. Then when you are ready to fit, remove the entire assembly, and coat the mold with Tacky Wax. Return the crown and branch set to the form. Fit the glass pieces to the mold and make final adjustments. Remove the glass pieces, foil, and replace on form. You may need to place small balls of Tacky Wax under pieces close to the branches and crown to improve appearance and decrease the gap between metal and foiled pieces. Each piece abutting the metal crown and branches should be tacked and tinned along with the rest of the lamp As mentioned earlier, when bead soldering the pieces next to the crown, the entire circumference should be soldered at one time. The larger metal masses create a heat sink that is impossible to bead when cold. It may be helpful to use a large soldering iron (150 watts) to facilitate soldering. Very careful heating with a small propane torch may be necessary but use caution. *Apply the heat only to the bronze crown and avoid overheating to prevent heat fractures of the glass pieces.*

(b) Worden:

Worden produces a tree limb filigree similar to the original on Tiffany lamps. It is divided into five sections and is compatible with the sectional forms used for constructing the Wisteria, Grape Vine, Pendent Cherry Tree and the Trumpet Vine lamps. A smaller cast filigree divided into three sections fits the Miniature Wisteria, Miniature Cherry Tree and Begonia lamps.

The brass casting needs to be thoroughly cleaned with hot water, detergent and fine steel wool. Tinning is recommended. Coat generously with paste flux. Use either a large soldering iron (150 watts) or a small propane torch to heat the metal sufficiently so the solder will flow and provide a thin smooth coating. A smaller soldering iron (60 – 100 watts) with a little tip may be helpful in spreading the solder into all the small openings. After the filigree is completely tinned, rinse and dry.

When you are ready to start assembling your lamp section, begin by placing the cast filigree on the form in the designated area. It is held in place with pins. The glass pieces abutting the brass filigree sometimes need to be modified in order to improve fit. You may want to place a pin into the form underneath a glass piece to raise it slightly and decrease the gap between metal and foiled piece. Each piece on the section should be tacked and tinned. Complete each section and proceed with joining the sections. The 'Two Form Method' of assembly is recommended (described on page 10 of the *Worden Instructional Manual*, 1990.

4. Finishing

a. Cleaning

After the bead soldering is completed, the lamp will need to be thoroughly cleaned to remove all traces of flux. As the lamp was soldered, most of the Tacky Wax has already vaporized or melted off, especially if continually wiped with a soft towel.

If a brass ring and rim was used in constructing your lamp, excess solder needs to be filed down to the brass and the edge blended into the bead. The top of the ring should also be filed down to the brass and the inside and lower surface of the ring completely cleaned of any solder. All filed surfaces are then sanded with 120 grit emery paper to remove any file marks and smooth the surface. This can be followed by 200 grit if you want it to be very smooth.

Apply a chlorinated cleanser (Comet®, Ajax®, etc) and *scrub* thoroughly. When you are through, the shade should be 'squeaky' clean. The chlorinated cleanser contains pumice; it imparts a 'tooth' to the metal, making it more receptive to patina. Rinse thoroughly with clean water and dry with soft cloths or towels.

b. Patina

The art of applying a patina or aged appearance to the metal surface of your lamp can be difficult and exacting. It is beyond the scope of this chapter to discuss specific chemical formulae, however, there are a number of commercial patinas available. **Caution should be exercised when using patinas. All should be considered toxic to skin, eyes and the respiratory tract. Read cautions on the product carefully; use only in a well-ventilated area and wear rubber gloves, a properly fitted OSHA approved mask and protective clothing.** If you notice that the patina is spotty and uneven in reacting with the metal, the lamp needs to be re-cleaned. If there is significant oxidation on the metal, it may need to be thoroughly cleaned with very fine steel wool.

It may be helpful to purchase your lamp base or hanging hardware before applying the patina to the lampshade. You will want to duplicate the finish as closely as possible so the two finishes match.

(1) Black Patina

This is the simplest and most frequently used metal finish for stained glass projects. It usually contains nitric acid and selenius dioxide. There are a number of commercially available black patinas carried by most stained glass suppliers. Before applying the patina solution, it may be helpful to warm the lamp with hot tap water, or place the lamp over a 100 watt bulb for about 20 minutes, or use a hair dryer. Work rapidly and apply the liquid patina all over the lamp (not just the soldered lines). As soon as the appropriate color is reached (usually a shade of gray), rinse generously with hot tap water. Now apply patina to the interior of the lamp and rise. Blot dry using old towels and rags.

(2) Copper Patina

This finish is a little more difficult to achieve than the one with black patina. Copper patina solution contains copper sulfate and is readily available either as a solution or as crystals which are usually mixed with hot water. In either case, follow directions carefully. Copper sulfate will not affect brass, and if brass ring, rim or filigree are used, they will need to be tinned prior to applying patina. After the final cleaning, the copper sulfate solution is applied and often re-applied several times until there is a copper appearance. Heating the lamp does not seem to hasten the patina. This process imparts a *very thin* layer of copper on the lamp.

The copper finish can be left as it is, polished with a non-abrasive copper polish for a shiny copper finish or additional chemicals can be applied to create a 'Tiffany' appearance. (See 4.d, Applying Patina to a Copper Plated Lamp)

c. Copper Plating

Tiffany wanted to have a uniform metal finish on his lamps and bases. Because brass, copper, tin and lead respond differently to patinas, he elected to have the lamps electroplated with copper. Then, the patina was applied. Today, electroplating is still recommended for providing the best patina for your lamp. It is often difficult to find a company with experience in plating stained glass lamps. Your local stained glass retailer may be helpful, or you may consult the Yellow Pages™ under 'Plating.' The usual cost varies from $50 to $100 depending on the size of the shade.

d. Applying Patina to a Copper Plated Lamp

After retrieving your lamp from the plater it will have a pink, hazy appearance. It will need to be cleaned thoroughly with a chlorinated cleanser to remove all fingerprints and smudges. Then, the patina is applied using brushes or rags. Although there are commercially available solutions, they are not readily available. Check with your retail stained glass supplier for patina solutions for bronze, brass and copper. Both American DeRosa® and Jax® have a line of patinas available with shades ranging from browns to grays and including greens. Commercial lamp manufacturers usually dip or immerse their metals into a bath of chemicals and guard the exact formulae and methods for achieving a particular color or appearance.

Expect to experiment to some extent when applying the patinas, because there is considerable variability to the manner in which chemicals react with metals. An effective approach has been to use a dark brown patina applied generously with a brush. Warming the lamp with either hot tap water or a hair dryer prior to application tends to speed the process of coloration. If the patina is too dark, use extremely fine steel wool to remove some of the color and add highlights. After you have achieved the look you want, rinse with water and pat dry (do not use soaps at this time as you may damage the finish). You may apply a Tiffany Green patina at this point; it is usually slower to react with the metal than the other finishes and will need to be applied in multiple coats allowing drying in between coats to build up a blue-green encrustation. Warming does not seem to speed the process.

Finally, if a patina is close but not exactly what you want, consider using acrylic paint to add highlights of reddish brown or blue-green. Using a paint sparingly to add highlights can dramatically improve the appearance, and it is often the only way to achieve a close match with a particular finish on a lamp base.

The important thing to remember when applying a patina to your lamp is patience. If you become too frustrated, clean the lamp with a soft rag or brush and a little soap (Jolt®), wait a couple of days, and try again. Or you can call the Odyssey Hotline (800) 228-2631.

After you have achieved the look you want, handle carefully. Do not use soaps or abrasives to clean the lamp. To protect the finish, you can apply paste wax (2–3 coats) and buff with a cloth. The best protection is achieved by spraying the shade, including the glass and all metal parts, with nitrocellulose lacquer (not acrylic). However, lacquer can be difficult to apply as it must be applied with a paint sprayer, **it also is toxic and requires safety precautions.** It may peel unless applied correctly. So, if you have the experience and equipment, spray the lamp; otherwise apply wax, polish and enjoy.

5. Final Operation
Alastair Duncan (Reprinted with permission)

When you have assembled a lampshade either with lead came or copper foil, soldered it neatly, applied an antiquing agent, and scrubbed and polished both the leading and the glass so that the lamp is sparkling clean and neat, you have arrived, finally, at the last stage; i.e., that of finishing it. This entails fitting it on to a base or hanging it, wiring it, selecting your preferred light wattage; and, lastly signing it.

These last stages are typically the ones to which the least attention is paid by the glass exponent, who, sensing victory, rushes to complete his masterpiece. It is a strange fact that a person who will spend many hours diligently designing, cutting leading, and soldering a lamp will often sacrifice all the patience and expertise that he has shown up until this stage—in the sudden urgency of trying to finish it—by hanging the lamp just any old how, by fitting the first bulb he finds no matter how powerful or weak it is, and, in general, ignoring all the rules of aestheticism that he applied so conscientiously to assembling the glass. Some people have the feeling that, because they do not themselves make the lamp fittings and bases as they did the lamp itself, that the latter are by this fact somehow outside their control or responsibility, and not an integral part of the final lamp. This is, needless to say, a false premise, for if the lamp is not tastefully displayed, then all the artist's virtuosity has been in vain. The ultimate success of the lamp does, therefore, hinge on the finishing operation. In the same way that an ill-chosen picture-frame can ruin a beautiful painting, so too with lamp fittings—they significantly add to or detract from the end-effect.

Lampshades are generally displayed by one of two methods: either on a base as a table lamp or by a chain or wall bracket as a hanging lamp. The decorative considerations and electrical components required for the two are, in part, the same, but there are certain differences, and we will for this reason, discuss them separately.

a. Table lamps
There are several considerations to selecting a base to support the lampshades. *First,* the most important, is the size ratio of the base to the shade—the height and thickness of the base vis-a-vis the diameter of the shade. There are no hard and fast rules here other than to try the two together to see whether they fit. Some bases contain a rod and screw mechanism to make them adjustable heightwise, and this greatly increases the range of shade sizes that these bases can accommodate.

Secondly, base style. Here the choice of base is a personal one, but there are certain aesthetic guidelines. Do not, for example, fit an ornate, rococo base to a modern shade, as this is obviously incongruous. Try always to match the two by artistic style; yet again, a very fussy base should not be matched with a similarly busy shade as the former will complete with the latter. In such a case, the base should be unpretentiously functional to highlight the intricacy of the shade.

Thirdly, base material. Brass, bronze, and iron are the most common materials for bases as they have the solidity and structural strength needed to support the combined weight of the glass and solder. Bases made of aluminum and lighter metals or alloys, will topple at the slightest touch.

Fourthly, colour harmony. You should, if possible, match the colour of the base with the solder on the shade. If you have applied a bronze patina to the solder then the base should, ideally, be of a similar colour. Likewise, a black finish on the solder should be complemented by a dark base. An easier way of matching the two is to finish the shade in the colour of the base, thereby eliminating the time and energy to re-colour the latter, but if you do need to change the base, then there are antiquing solutions on the market, such as patinas and lacquers, which can be applied.

Other components of a table lamp are:

Electrical fittings: These usually fit on, or near the top of the base shaft, and consist of either a single or a cluster of sockets—the manner of attachment depending on how the shade is connected to the base. The number of bulbs to use requires both an artistic and a functional consideration, with a cluster tending to disperse the light more evenly than a single one. It is much better to use two or three bulbs of lower wattage than a single high one as the latter tends to concentrate the light far too strongly on only one area of the shade.

The electrical link from the socket(s) to the source of power, usually a wall-plug, is by means of a cord that passes down through the inside of the base, (all lamp bases should contain a central, hollow passage for this purpose) and then emerges near or on the pedestal. Finally, the on-off switch can be placed at various points; on the wall, on the cord, or by means of a chain attachment on certain sockets. Remember, again, to try to choose a cord of a colour which will blend with the overall appearance of the shade and base.

Shade attachment: Various bases employ different methods of supporting the shade; the two most common are a harp mechanism or a rod that extends up from the bottom of the base through the electrical fittings to secure the shade at the centre at the top. The various components—such as screws, nuts, and nipples—necessary to complete the link-up are always carried by a supplier of electrical lamp fittings.

Vase caps, spiders, and finials: If the top aperture of the shade is circular, then it is usually best secured by two vase caps; which form the top and give the shade a decorative finish. One is on the inside and the other on the outside of the glass, with the former supporting the shade from underneath and the latter both holding it in place, . These vase caps should be of the same size and be only fractionally larger than the opening so that they hold the shade securely while covering as little as possible of the glass that you so laboriously cut and leaded up— the purpose of which is, after all, that it be seen. If, however, the aperture is not circular but, for example, square or polygonal, or if the lamp has a crown, then circular vase caps cannot effectively be used, and you should use some other form of attachment such as a spider or iron crossbar. A spider consists of a central nut from which several arms protrude horizontally. The rod in the lamp base passes through the nut and the arms of the spider must first be measured and then cut off with a saw so that they can be soldered on to the edges of the top opening of the shade.

Lastly, on the very top of the table lamp, comes the finial. This is the nut into which the nipple (threaded pipe) protruding through the vase caps, either on the end of the base rod or on the harp attachment, is screwed to hold the composition of base and shade together. Finials are offered in a range of shapes from a purely functional nut to much more elaborate designs that act as a decorative fillip to the lamp as a whole.

b. Hanging Lamps
Components:

These vary in some respects from those used in a table lamp, and I will describe them starting from the top and moving downward.

Ceiling caps: These are manufactured in various sizes and designs and are screwed into the electrical box fitting in the ceiling to both neatly cover the aperture where the wiring protrudes from the box and to support the combined weight of the chain and the shade. Ceiling caps are made of brass or bronze and have a hollow hook through which the electrical cord passes and on to which the top link of the chain is attached. In the event that the aperture on the ceiling is not situated directly above where you wish to hang your lamp, then an additional, smaller ceiling cap—in effect, only a hook—should be screwed into the ceiling at the required point, and then the chain

is swaged from the larger cap to the hook, from where it hangs vertically. Swaging is not only functional in that the wire, and hence electricity, can be relayed from the central point to any part of the room, but it can be highly decorative, with gentle loops of chain providing the lampshade with very elegant support.

The chain: There are any number of chains available, varying in size and design of link. Try, when making your selection, to match the colour and style of the chain with that of the lamp. They should balance.

The one end of the chain fits onto the hook on the ceiling cap while the other end fits onto the metal loop on the lamp. Chains are made in various lengths and can, in addition, be shortened or extended by the supplier to meet your needs.

Metal loop: This has two purposes: that of connecting the chain to the lamp and that of securing the nipple that protrudes through the holes in the vase cap from the inside of the lamp. A metal loop differs from a finial in that it has a hollow central passage to allow the electrical cord to pass through it to be connected to the light socket below. Various shapes and sizes are available.

Vase caps: These should be selected with the same considerations of style and sizes as those for table lamps. Remember that lamps that contain crowns cannot use vase caps and must, instead, be hung with a spider or crossbar.

Nipples: These are threaded pipes that, on the one end, screw into the light socket and, on the other into the metal loop on the top of the shade. They are made in various lengths and widths, and can, in addition, be cut with a saw when necessary.

Light Sockets: These, like those on table lamps, vary in shape, size and design; common varieties being made of brass, bakelite, and porcelain. The choice of whether to purchase them with or without an on-off chain or a pull-push switch is a personal one—with functionality being the determinate. Larger shades require clusters or two, three, or four light sockets to diffuse the light evenly.

Wiring a hanging lamp: The cord is fed through the ceiling cap, down the chain, through the metal loop and nipple, and, finally, into the light socket. I recommend that you feed the cord through every third or so link in the chain, making certain that it is always longer than the chain so that it is at no stage supporting the weight of the shade. Check, while doing this, that none of the links are enmeshed so that no sudden link slippage can occur with might break the cord or force it out of the socket.

Hanging lamps: How best to display them.

Ceiling or wall lamps do, if fixed above eye-level, present a problem in that you can see inside them. Not only the bulb, but everything else that goes to make up the

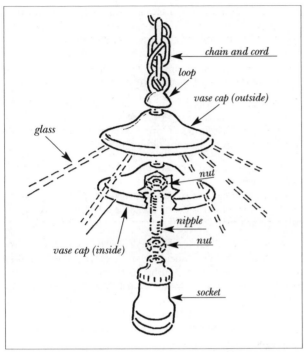

Figure 21.17 Diagrammatic representation of the fittings for a typical hanging lamp

undercarriage of the shade - the socket, nipple, nuts, etc. —will be visible, none of which are intended to be eye-catching but which often are, for exactly the wrong reasons. Not only do such electrical fittings detract from the overall beauty of the lamp, but the viewer sees the inner surface of the glass by the glare of the reflected light rays of the bulb, and not from the outside surface by transmitted light as it should be seen for maximum effect.

One sees all too may hanging lamps, that one can only assume are beautiful, hung or fixed to a wall bracket so high up that, while all of their insides can be seen, only the lower inch or so of the outside of the lamp skirt is visible. To remedy this one should either extend the length of the chain from which the lamp is hanging or turn the lamp bottom side up and fasten it directly to the ceiling or the the chain. There is, in this respect, no one correct method of hanging a lamp; the only criterion being that as much of the glass that you wish to be seen, is, in fact. Most shades, especially hemispheres or dome-shaped ones, can be at least as attractive when hung upside down as when they are right side up. A glass lamp's unique attraction is in the luminosity of the glass when backlit, so the higher the lamp is positioned above eye-level and the less of the outside of the glass that can be seen if it is hung in the conventional way, i.e., with its crown upwards, then the less decorative it will be.

An alternative method of alleviating this problem, but one that I feel is less satisfactory, is to use a large frosted

Duralite® globe instead of a standard one. A globe both softens the glare of the naked bulb and, because of its large spherical shape, obscures the electrical fittings above it, thereby making the best of a bad show. Globes are made with a top metal holder that contains three thumb screws which, when screwed inward, hold the globe in position, and which, when screwed outward, release the globe, thereby enabling you to change the bulb when necessary. The complete globe unit is sold in various sizes that, however, require a special device which can be obtained from an electrical supply shop to link them on to standard lamp fittings. The extra effort is, though, more than compensated for by their neat appearance.

Filigree Borders, collars: These are very specialized items usually only stocked by stained glass suppliers and which, when used with discretion, can add that extra, sometimes indefinable, touch of quality to either a table or hanging lamp. Their over-use, however, will drastically cheapen it, as too much filigree has a decidedly 'kitsch' look about it.

Filigreed borders and collars are staple bands of metal, usually brass or lead, that are used either, or both, to hide joints which, because they are sharply angular, are difficult to solder neatly or to be superimposed as an ornamental overlay on the glass.

These borders are pressed from very thin material and are, therefore, malleable and can be wrapped and tacked (soldered) on to the joints along the entire bottom edge of a lamp to give it an ornate finish. They are best used in shades that have large panels of a single colour at they will obviously both obscure and detract from any linear design in the glass over which they are positioned.

To attach either a border or a collar, wrap them around the glass as tightly as you can and then mark the point where the end and the beginning meet. Next, carefully cut off the end with metal shears so that the two edges of the resulting joint are flush. Then rub the area of the joint very gently with a wire brush to remove any oxidation on the metal, flux it, and apply as little solder as necessary to bond the two ends together. (You will best solicit an extra pair of hands for this operation to prevent the two ends from slipping). The less conspicuous the joint, the tidier it will be. Finally, add an antiquing agent to the entire filigree to give it a uniform colour, thereby further disguising the joint.

Filigree bands that form the lower border of a lamp can, in addition, be drilled or punched with holes into which various pendants can be hooked by wire. Fringes such as glass prisms, crystals, and strings of beads are some such items.

c. Lighting considerations for lamps

As a general rule, I would recommend that the more transparent the glass in the lamp, the lower the wattage of the globe used. Conversely, the less transparent the glass, the brighter the bulb can be. You can, in addition, experiment with the wide range of bulbs — frosted and coloured now commercially available. There are, also, numerous lighting devices, such as dimmer switches, rheostats, and other light modulators, which can be regulated form a wall-switch to produce any number of changeable colour effects and moods.

d. Signature

For some inexplicable reason, most people who would not hesitate to have their names emblazoned proudly across a painting would not, however, consider signing their creations in glass, and such illogicality is not lessened by the fact that it is difficult to make one's mark, so to speak, neatly and permanently on lead or glass without the proper tools. There are, though, three good reasons against anonymity in your work. First, your signature gives it a personal and professional finish by adding that extra little something to show your pride in the finished object. Secondly, and related to this, you will find that the fact that you know that you will finally affix your name to the end product acts as a form of psychological quality control that will discourage you from allowing any shoddy workmanship to go uncorrected. This applies particularly to messily soldered joints that you tend to promise yourself, in all good faith, that you will return to later, but which, somehow, you invariably never quite get to do. Thirdly, you will find that if and when you decide to sell what you have made, that most buyers do, and indeed should, expect that it be signed. An autographed object of art is a far better potential investment to a purchaser than one that is not, which, in turn, if nothing else, often helps to narrow the gap between what you and he feels your creation is worth price-wise!

There are basically two ways of signing a leaded glass object: either on the glass or on the leading. The former is best done with a scriber specially designed for this purpose. It has a stylus which enables you to scratch you name or monogram into the surface of the glass. Be careful, though, when using it, not to apply too much pressure or to make your signature too big because a scriber performs the same function as glass wheel cutter (they are both made of tungsten carbide) in that it actually scores the glass, so too much force could generate a fracture.

The method of applying your signature to the soldering can be done in similar fashion by carving into the surface of the lead came or soldered copper foil, but I do not recommend this as it is impermanent and looks amateurish. The oxidation of the lead or the darkening effect of an antiquing agent, if you are using one, will tend to cause the lettering to fade into its background. It can, in addition, be inadvertently or intentionally filed off the surface of the leading. No, the best procedure is to order a batch of copper or brass name tags, about ⅛″ wide with your name inscribed on them, from a sign-maker. These can be fluxed and soldered onto the leading to form a permanent and very professional finish to your projects. The conventional position for these is, on lampshades, on the inside lower border leading of the skirt.

D. Neon
Carole Perry

There are many similarities inherent in tube bending and stained glass whether it be flat glass, fused glass, or other. The ultimate objective is to encourage interest and activity that will further explore the possibilities and applications in combining these elements.

1. The History of Neon

One of many common misunderstandings about 'neon lighting' is centered on its origins and French founder, Georges Claude. In 1910, Georges Claude exhibited the first sign using neon gas at the Grand Palais in Paris. The critical discovery was not the use of gas to generate light— this had been accomplished in the mid 1800's using common gases, nitrogen and carbon dioxide—but the development of a corrosion resistant electrode, which he patented in 1915, ensuring a near monopoly for the multi-million dollar Claude Neon Company. Hence, the widespread belief exists that neon lighting is the direct result of a man named 'Claude Neon.'

The second major misunderstanding resides in the term 'neon lights' which perpetuates the assumption 'lit by neon gas.' Luminous tubes, the proper term, are most commonly filled with either neon, which produces a brilliant orange-red color in clear tubing, or argon combined with vaporized mercury, which produces a brilliant blue (by itself, argon produces a soft violet color). Both are considered 'rare' gases, but are found in the air we breathe. Other applications, although truly rare and quite expensive, include the inert gases krypton and xenon.

In its heyday in the 1930s, over 5,000 tube benders were employed at more than 2,000 neon sign companies in the United States alone. These are startling statistics when you consider the first neon sign was installed in Los Angeles in 1924, barely ten years earlier. The first two signs were purchased for $1,200 each from the Claude Neon Company by automobile dealer, Earle Anthony, for his Packard showroom. One of Anthony's signs was still operational in 1977, long after the last Packard graced an automobile showroom. The phenomenal growth of the neon business is attributed to a number of factors.

My personal pick for the number one contribution to neon's rapid ascent is color, color and color. Colored lights are as compelling today as ever. Doesn't gridlock occur in even the smallest American towns each time the word gets out that someone has created an overwhelming Christmas light display? A great variety of color, coupled with previously unseen brilliance and sparkle, in the dreariest weather imaginable—there could be no doubt that neon lights were destined for success.

Georges Claude had some very strong sales support as well. Charles Lindbergh, after his celebrated transatlantic flight, was paid by Claude Neon to act as their public relations agent in the U.S. The benefits, beyond the attention grabbing novelty that Lindbergh could list, were many. Of greatest importance to the advertiser and sign industry were, and still are, that luminous neon tubes (vs. incandescent lights)

a. require far less power,

b. produce much more light, and

c. offer a three-dimensional flexibility that is limited only by one's imagination.

In the 80 plus years that have passed since Claude's discovery, virtually nothing of significance has changed in the technical process of neon fabrication. The original text book of the '40s, *Neon Techniques and Handling: Handbook of Neon Signs and Cold Cathode Lighting*, by Samuel C. Miller, is still the only text book available, and it's instruction is still technically current and accurate.

What has changed, dramatically, is the number of active skilled benders available to perform a craft that requires years to master. In the early 1980's, only 200–300 remained, with most of those past retirement age. Today, the number of newly trained glass benders has increased sharply to meet the new demand for exposed neon in both the sign and decorator business. We can only hope that the quality of much of the neon work being installed today improves rapidly enough to prevent another decline in the industry. A properly executed neon sign should burn for 50 years or better.

2. Creating a Neon Sign:

Before beginning, a tube bender needs certain materials and tools. A pattern is the first item required. The pattern must be measured with a map-measuring wheel to determine the length of glass tubing required for the job; the pattern must be studied to determine the best starting point and the type of bends required to effectively complete the piece. There may be a dozen ways to bend the tubes to create a simple 'OPEN' sign, but only one or two will minimize the length of tube required, the amount of block-out paint needed for the spaces between letters, and the size of the transformer required to power the neon.

Glass tubing, commonly referred to as 'sticks' are used. The sticks generally come in 4-foot lengths, but the diameter varies from 9–25 millimeters. 10–15 millimeters is most frequently used. While the choice of colors is still around 40, many of the original colored glasses have been replaced with clear glass tubes that are coated with fluorescent powders. It is the interaction of the gases with this powder that creates the different colors.

Ultimately, electrodes will be needed (spliced to the ends of the tubes), neon, argon, or other rare gas, block-out paint, and the proper size transformer. The minimum required equipment includes:

• burners, to soften the glass for bending and splicing,

• a pumping system, which includes a bombarder and manifold, to remove the undesired gas and impurities from inside the tube as well as to insert the rare gas.

a. Six basic steps to creating a 'neon' sign.

1) Heat the sticks over a flame (i.e., cross fire, ribbon burner) to soften the glass. Choose the burner based on the particular bend. If, for example, for a circle for the letter 'O', use an open ribbon burner to soften a longer section of the glass. For a right angle bend, place the stick in the cross fires. When a color change or additional tubing needs to be added, use a hand torch to splice the two sticks together.

2) Bend the glass to match the design pattern drawn on non-asbestos material, (the recent replacement for asbestos sheets). Bend the glass stick and then move from the fire to the pattern, place the hot piece onto the pattern to assure proper alignment. Mark the next bend with chalk while the previous bend cools.

3) Weld the electrodes on each end of the completed tube, again using the hand torch. It is the electrode that carries the electrical charge from the transformer to the gas

4) Attach the finished piece to the manifold (pumping system) with the hand torch to:

    a.) Clean: bombard the inside with up to 30,000 volts of electricity,

    b.) Vacuum: remove the air and impurities,

    c.) Fill: replace vacuum with the inert gas.

5) Seal off (again with the hand torch) the finished tube, and

6) Connect a transformer to the tube to 'age' or burn in the tube, bringing it to its proper level of light.

This process cannot be hurried, short cut, or automated. On a good day, perhaps five or six or even a dozen relatively simple signs (i.e., the words 'Chevron' or 'California'), might be produced from start to finish with no help. On a great day, with assistance performing functions 4–6, 75 border units might easily be produced. But on a bad day, one flamingo might require a second day.

3. Combining Luminous Tubes and Fused Glass

Living in the Southwest, most of our designs have Southwest themes in which the neon is integrated into fused designs. My husband John does the neon, and I do the fusing. We have done many free-standing pieces of native animals and Native American themes, combining the two techniques. On the contemporary side, we've mixed abstract neon tubes with free-form woven glass strings, mounting them on black plexiglas, a common surface for neon wall sculpture. The mounted surface becomes a 'box' that allows for hidden placement of the transformer (the necessary power source) and wiring.

a.) Technical Problems

We have bonded our work with a variety of substances—silicone, epoxy, ultraviolet adhesive—everything but the most obvious method, fusing, because there are a number of technical problems.

1) Glass slumps at a lower temperature than it fuses. In the kiln, the glass tube will collapse before it can fuse to the additional glass.

2) Application of the glass outside the kiln, using the burners and keeping air pressure in the tube, has inherent handling difficulties, which if overcome, would still result in the application fracturing due to thermal gradient.

3) Incompatibility between standard neon tubing and the glass used for the design work.

None of these problems are impossible to overcome. Air expands as it is heated, so it remains to be discovered how much air (or gas?) should be sealed in a tube before it can be kiln fused to another piece of glass without losing its shape to expansion or sagging. Blowing our own luminous tubes from compatible glass, or creating flat glass designs from fused colored neon tubes are both options to overcoming compatibility problems.

The possibilities of neon are expanding faster than one can even write about them. Less than five years ago, there were no more than forty color variations available by combining different gases with tinted or coated tubes. Soon I anticipate there will be twice that. Tomorrow, who knows?

The potential of neon in glass art and sculpture is virtually untapped. It is three dimensional, shadowless and kinetic, offering the opportunity to draw with light. It is the ultimate enhancement to multimedia art. Rather than being forced to position your work against sunlight or someone else's artificial light plan, we can incorporate the light into the glass. We can control how our work is viewed, include the audience as participants, from the point of creation.

Areas to explore include the use of controlled air bubbles that we can convert to neon light sources. Our respective studios and home are filled with designs, some functional and some pure art forms, that combine glass, gas and electricity. Our ultimate goal would be to have a home that is completely and adequately lighted without a single incandescent bulb. More than possible, it is extremely practical, and with measurable energy savings.

E. Bibliography

Duncan, Alastair, Martin Eiddlelberg, Neil Harris. *Master Works of Louis Comfort Tiffany*. New York: Abrams, 1989.

Duncan, Alastair. *Tiffany at Auction*. New York: Rizzoli, 1981.

-----. *Tiffany Windows*. New York: Simon and Schuster, 1980.

Feldstein, William, Jr. and Alastair Duncan. *The Lamps of Tiffany Studios*. New York: Abrams, 1983.

French, Jennie. *Glass Works, The Copper Foil Technique of Stained Glass*. New York: Van Nostrand Reinhold, 1974.

General Electric Company, *Light and Color*. TP-ll9, Apr., 1989.

—. "Specifying Light and Color," *Lighting Application Bulletin*. n.d.

Isenberg, Anita and Seymour. *Stained Glass Lamps Construction and Design*. Chilton, PA: 1974.

Koch, Robert. *Louis C. Tiffany's Glass, Bronzes, and Lamps*. New York: Crown, 1971.

La Giusa, Frank F. and Douglas Phillips. "Guides for Nighttime Lighting of Windows in Stained Glass or Plastic," *Illuminating Engineering*, Journal of the Illuminating Engineering Society, (March 1971).

Lakich, Lili. *Neon Lovers Glow in the Dark*. CA: Museum of Neon Art, 1986.

Luciano. *Stained Glass Lamps and Terrariums*. CA: Hidden House, 1973.

McKean, Hugh F. *The Lost Treasures of Louis Comfort Tiffany*. New York: Doubleday, 1980.

Miller, Samuel. *Neon Techniques and Handling: Handbook of Neon Signs and Cold Cathode Lighting*. 3rd ed., Cincinnati, OH: Signs of the Times Publishing, 1977.

Neustadt, Egon. *The Lamps of Tiffany*. New York: Fairfield Press, 1970.

Paul, Tessa. *The Art of Louis Comfort Tiffany*. New York: Exeter Books, 1987.

Phillips, Douglas and Frank F. LaGiusa. "Lighting and Stained Glass," *Light Magazine*, Vol. 39, No. 3, 1971. General Electric Company.

Porter, Norman and Douglas Jackson. *Tiffany Glassware*. New York: Crown, 1988.

Stern, Rudi. *Let There be Neon*. New York: Abrams, 1979.

-----. *The New Let There be Neon*. Revised Edition, New York: Abrams, 1988.

Webb, Michael. *The Magic of Neon*. 2nd ed., Layton, UT: Gibbs M. Smith, Inc., 1986.

Appendix A
Glossary

Lucy Enos, Dawn Sinkovich, Susan Osborn

Abrade (Abrasion)
To scrape away the surface of glass to remove the colored layer of *flashed glass* with an iron point file, wheel or bit,.

Abrasive
Any substance used for grinding, cutting, polishing, or carving, as in 'abrasive etching.'

Abstract Design
1. A design whose forms have been reduced or modified from representational forms. 2. A design using non-representational forms.

Accelerator
See *Activator, Catalyst and Hardener.*

Acetates
Scaled color designs on clear film that simulate the effect of stained glass.

Acetone
A flammable chemical solvent used as a cleaning fluid.

A.C.G.I.H.
American Conference of Governmental Industrial Hygienists.

Acid
A substance that will redden litmus paper; a compound containing hydrogen replaceable by positive elements or radicals to form salts; a compound that dissociates in a water solution with the production of hydrogen ions; a compound or ion that gives protons (hydrogen ions) to some other substance.

Acid Badgering
Lightly etching or frosting the glass surface with an acid etching cream.

Acid Cut Back
A preparation step in cameo carving to remove excess glass from the background of the design to be carved in high relief.

Aciding—Acid Etching
The process of etching the thin layer of color off the surface of flashed glass with hydrofluoric acid to allow the base color to show through. The process may be also be used on clear glass to produce a semi-opaque carved result.

Acid Polishing
Chemical polishing of glass using concentrated sulphuric and hydrofluoric acid solutions.

Acid Proof
Unaffected by acid contact.

Acid Resist
Material used to resist the etching action in the etching process.

Acid Resistant
Withstands the action of acid. See *Acid Proof.*

Action Level (lead exposure)
Employee exposure level without the use of respirators, to an airborne concentration of lead measured per cubic meter of air averaged over an 8-hour period.

Activator
See *Accelerator, Catalyst, Hardener.*

Active
The part of the window that is moveable. It may be indicated on a blueprint by an X.

Aerosol Sprayer
Container of gas under pressure used as a propellant.

Agar Solution
A material used for wetting metal surfaces for suspending enamels.

Aggregate
Inert granular material.

Air Brush
A small version of the spray gun, capable of being used as an artist's tool.

Aisle
In large churches, the area parallel to the nave, one aisle on either side of the nave—hence the aisle windows.

Alabaster
A hard, translucent mineral, when sliced thin, was glazed into plaster grille work to allow light into dwellings (pre-stained glass) in dryer climates.

Alabaster Glass
A type of milk white glass that traps light as does opalescent glass but with a warm, soft sheen.

Alexandrite
A glass that appears one color in artificial light and another color in natural light.

Alkali Cleaners
Strong alkaline cleaners such as trisodium phosphate.

Alkaline Solution
A base or hydroxide solution of a soluble mineral salt or mixture of salts. Alkaline solutions are capable of neutralizing acids.

Alkali Resistant
Withstands the action of alkaline solutions, such as detergents. See *Detergent Resistant.*

Alloy
Different metals combined and completely intermixed forming a new metal with unique properties.

Alumina Hydrate $Al_2O_3 \cdot 3H_2O$
A fine white powder made from bauxite, a major ingredient in shelf primer. See *Kiln Wash, Shelf Primer.*

Aluminum Design Foil
An adhesive backed foil made for cutting positive and negative stencils.

Aluminum Oxide Al_2O_3
A common abrasive used in abrasive etching glass, also called alumina, 9 on Mohs Value of Hardness.

Amber Stain
See *Silver Stain.*

Ambient Light
The existing, diffused light. Light coming from many directions.

Ambulatory
The aisle circling the eastern or apse end of the church behind the altar.

Analogous Colors
Colors close to each other on the color wheel.

Anchor
Any device used to secure the window to the building.

Aniline Dye
Any synthetic pseudo-organic dye.

Anneal
The controlled cooling of glass to relieve internal stress.

Annealing Oven
A kiln used to heat and slowly cool glass. See *Lehr.*

Annealing Point
The temperature at which the internal stresses in glass are reduced to an acceptable limit, usually 35° F to 40° F above the strain point.

Annealing Range
The temperature range at which glass is held to allow the release of stress. The upper end is the annealing point. The lower end is the strain point.

Anneal Soak
The stage in cooling glass where the temperature is held constant for a period of time to relieve stress.

Anodize
To subject a metal, as the anode, to electrolytic action in order to create an oxidized film or coating.

Antique Glass
Mouth blown sheet glass with the irregularity of 'medieval' glass. Glass blown into a large cylinder that is cut, opened, and flattened into a sheet. Variations of antique glass may include seedy, crackle, flashed, opal, opak, reamy and streaky. 'Antique' refers to the technique—not the age. See *Mouth Blown Glass.*

Applied Decoration
Small pieces of molten glass added as decoration to the main gather.

Appliqué
Adhering stained glass to a substrate with epoxy or other adhesives.

Apse
The semi-circular termination of the east end of the chancel or chapel.

Aqua Regia
A mixture of hydrochloric acid and nitric acid used to dissolve gold and platinum.

Aqueous
A solution made with water.

Architectural Glass
Stained glass designed, made, and installed to harmonize with the structure and function of a building.

Armature
A metal divisional bar or bars making a framework for supporting stained glass, usually fixed into a wall. Also used within concrete for strengthening.

Arrissing
The process of removing sharp edges from glass.

Art Deco
The style of work produced in the early twentieth century that reached its apex at the 'Exposition Internationale des Arts Décoratifs et Industriels Modernes' held in Paris in 1925. Characterized by bold geometric shapes, streamlined and rectilinear forms.

Art Glass
Art Nouveau—Victorian era stained glass using opalescent glass and enamel painting on glass.

Art Nouveau
French for 'The New Art,' an art movement popular in the 1890s and early 1900s in Europe and America. A busy, decorative style characterized by flowing vines and flat shapes (as seen in Tiffany glass,) and undulating lines.

Asbestos
A fireproof material now considered dangerous due to its classification as a carcinogen.

Ashlar
A type of design that uses brick-like shapes in even or random patterns.

Asphaltus Varnish
A liquid preparation used as a resist on glass when using hydrofluoric acid.

Atmosphere
The prevailing condition of the air in the kiln during firing.

Atom
The smallest particle of an element.

Aureole
A radiant light around a head or body of the representation of a sacred person.

Autonomous Panel
A non-architectural stained glass composition.

Aventurine
Glass with a sparkling appearance caused by the addition of metallic crystals to the melt.

Awning Window
A window whose sash is hinged at the top and projects out when open.

Background
The area of a window designed to emphasize a symbol or figure area.

Back-Painting
Painting on the back, or outer, surface of glass.

Back Up

Material placed in a joint to limit the depth of the sealant.

Badger Blender

A wide flat badger animal hair brush used to evenly spread matt paint on glass.

Badger Hair

The long hairs of the European badger, strong, pliable and quick drying. Used to make blenders that smooth out applied coatings of matting paint.

Bait

The tool dipped into molten glass to start the pulling operation.

Balance

1. A mechanical device used to counterbalance the sash when opening and closing a window. 2. A design with equal emphasis on opposite sides.

Ball Mill

A cylinder revolving on its axis with metal balls used to grind glass.

Balsam of Copaiba

A natural viscous, resinous liquid used as a color vehicle in decorating work.

Band

To decorate with bands or stripes while the object rotates.

Banding

Soldering copper wires to the lead came to hold the support bars.

Baptistery

A separate room or building of a church containing the font.

Banding Wheel

A revolving disk that turns the item to be banded.

Baptostru

A separate room or building of a church containing the baptismal font.

Bar/Barring

A solid metal bar, often steel, held by copper wire ties or solder directly to the interior of stained glass windows for support and reinforcement. See *Reinforcing Bar, Saddle Bar.*

Barcol Hardness

A measurement of the hardness of the part.

Baroque

1. Machine made to imitate reamy glass. 2. A style of art of seventeenth and eighteenth centuries characterized by overblown realism and curved figures.

Base Glass

The bottom layer of glass to which other glasses are fused, or the most common glass used.

Bat

A flat slab of material used as a base for construction of clay forms.

Batch

The raw materials needed to make glass, proportioned and mixed, ready for the glass furnace.

Batching Bin

The container in which raw materials for glass are mixed.

Bath

Submersion. A term applied to developing, fixing, or other photographic solutions; or an acid bath.

Battledore

A wooden paddle used by glass blowers.

Bauhaus

An artistic style derived from the principles of a German school of architecture and design founded in 1919, and terminated prior to World War II.

Bay

1. The space between columns. 2. One complete transverse unit of the architecture, interior or exterior.

Bay Window

Three or more window units attached to a building so as to project outward.

Bead

Any raised section extending around a piece of glass. Also, the raised solder line in copper foil work.

Beading

Laying an edge of solder over a copper foil seam.

Beeswax

After melting, used to secure glass pieces to a glass easel. See *Waxing Up.*

Bedding

The application of a compound in the setting channel when installing a panel.

Bending

The physical sagging or slumping of glass by heating in a kiln.

Bending Colors

Glass paints that are applied to flat glass, and fire onto the glass when it is slumped or bent.

Bent Glass

Sheet glass that has been sagged or curved over a form, in a kiln.

Bentonite

Principally aluminum silicate clays used in various adhesives, cements, ceramic fillers, and shelf primers.

Bevel

Cut and polished edge usually on plate glass at an angle other than 90°, done in stages with roughing, smoothing, cork and felt wheel polishing.

Beveling

The grinding and polishing of glass edges leaving a central raised section. Light is refracted through the beveled edges.

Bevel of Compound Bead

Caulking compound applied with a slant surface so water will drain away from the glass or panel.

Bezel

A flanged rim used to hold objects, such as jewels.

Biological Monitoring

Sampling and analysis of a person's blood samples for lead and zinc protoporphyrin levels, or other metabolic functions.

Birefringent

'Doubly refracting' glass with internal strains may show more than one refractive index relative to the direction of the traversing light.

Bisque Ware

Unglazed clay ware used as molds for slumping.

Bite

The amount of overlap between the glazing stop and the panel.

Black Patina

A chemical solution to color a solder surface black.

Blanchon

Shelf or tray for holding glass during firing.

Blank

Any piece of glass used for sagging, painting, fusing, etching or engraving that is cut to size and shape for a specific use.

Blasting Booth

A room used for sand carving, generally large enough for the operator to stand inside.

Blasting Cabinet

A bin used to protect the operator when abrasive etching or carving. The operator stands outside the cabinet, and reaches into the work area through gauntleted holes.

Blender

A brush usually made of badger hair used to evenly spread and smooth matting paint on glass.

Blending

The smoothing and distribution of wet matting paint, usually with a wide flat brush called a blender.

Blister

A bubble or imperfection that refracts the light coming through, considered desirable in antique glass, but a defect in commercial glass.

Block

A small piece of wood, lead or other material used to position the panel in the frame for glazing.

Blocking

1. The shaping of a gather of glass in a blocking mold. 2. Positioning a finished window evenly in its frame.

Blood Lead Levels

The amount of lead in a person's blood, usually expressed as micrograms of lead per 100 grams of whole blood. ($\mu g/dL$)

Blood ZZP Levels

The amount of zinc protoporphyrin in a person's blood. It is an metabolic indicator of the amount and character of the lead in the person's blood.

Bloom

A film produced when smoke and gases affect the surface of the glass.

Blow Mold

The metal mold in which a blown glass article is shaped.

Blown Glass

A technical process where glass is formed by blowing, as opposed to rolling or drawing.

Blow Over

A thin walled bubble formed above a hand blown mold to make it easier to crack off.

Blowpipe

A long hollow metal pipe on which a glassblower gathers molten glass from the furnace to be blown and shaped.

Body

1. The consistency of molten glass that makes it workable.
2. The main part of a design.

Bolting Cloth

A silk cloth of even mesh used for screening purposes.

Bond

To adhere glass to glass with adhesives or by firing.

Borate Glass

A glass formula in which boron oxide is used in place of silica.

Border

A narrow band of glass surrounding a window.

Borosilicate Glass

Specially formulated glass generally used as laboratory ware, characterized by low coefficient of expansion, and great resistance to thermal shock.

Boss

Small circular panel of ornament, normally set in the background of a window.

Bracketing

Taking a photograph at both one 'f' stop over and one 'f' stop under what seems to be the correct aperture setting.

Breaking the Score

Separating a piece of glass along a created score line. (See *Cutting Glass, Fracture, Score*)

Bridge

A flat board elevated on end blocks to support the hand above the glass while painting. Also called an arm rest.

Brilliant Cutting

The process of cutting or engraving on glass with a copper or stone wheel and abrasives.

Bristle

Bristle is the hair of the pig or hog. It is widely used in brushes, and is capable of delicate brushwork. It differs from the fur or hair of most other animals in that it does not come to a point, but ends in a group of finer filaments called the flag.

Glossary

B.T.U.
British Thermal Unit. The heat necessary to raise the temperature of one pound of water one degree Fahrenheit.

Bubble
An air pocket trapped in glass when it was in the molten state.

Bullseye
Raised mark left by the pontil during the process of making crown glass.

Bull's Eyes
The center of a piece of *crown glass* that includes the mark where the pontil was attached.

Burden, Total Body
See *Total Body Burden.*

Burnish
1. To polish by rubbing. 2. To rub down the edges of the stencil or copper foil to make them tight.

Buttering
Applying a thin layer of putty or sealant to the flat surface before installing a window.

Butt Joint
An intersection of two pieces of lead or other material which fit next to each other rather than overlapping or notching into each other.

Cadmium-selenide pigment
A group of pigments ranging in color from yellow orange through red to deep maroon, widely used in coloring glass paints. Somewhat fugitive in the firing, sensitive to kiln atmosphere, as well as extremes of temperature.

Calcine
To make powdery through the action of dry heat.

Calcium Carbonate (CaCO$_3$)
Whiting, a fine white powder used as a shelf primer and an absorbent for putty.

Came (Calms)
Metal strips, generally 'U' or 'H' shaped, used to hold glass pieces together to form a stained glass window. Originally lead, but zinc, brass copper and lead ores are also used. See *also Flange, Heart, Leaf.*

Camel Hair
Name for soft hair brushes, not actual camel hair, but sable, squirrel, pony hair, or mixture of the above. A mixed hair brush can be used for paints, but not for lusters.

Cameo Glass
A glass object, usually a vase, made up of multi layers of different colored glass cut away leaving a multicolored relief design.

Camera Ready
Art work that is ready for photo reproduction.

Campaign
The life of the tank or crucible of molten glass.

Cane
Thin glass rods either of single color or multi-color design, such as millefiori.

Cannon
See *Glass Cylinder.*

Canopy
An architectural framing device to enclose a figure or scene.

Carbon Tissue
A pigmentized gelatin-coated paper.

Carborundum Stone (Whetstone)
Carbide of silicon, an extremely hard abrasive used to smooth sharp edges of glass.

Carrara Glass
Flat glass containing crystals. See *Marbleized Glass.*

Carry-in Boy
The person who places the completed blown objects in the annealing lehr.

Cartoon
Full size working drawing showing detail of leading and painting.

Cartouche
Ornament in the form of a scroll, usually surrounding a medallion or text, associated with the Renaissance style.

Carving
To shape by cutting, engraving or abrasively etching into glass, to produce a three-dimensional image.

Cased Glass
A thin layer of colored glass applied over another layer of glass (generally clear). See *Flashed Glass.*

Casement Window
A window sash hung by hinges and fastened to the window frame.

Casping
Small protruding points of stone within areas of Gothic tracery.

Casting
Forming an object by pouring molten material in a mold.

Catalyst
A material used to activate thermoset plastic resins causing them to harden. See *Accelerator, Activator, Hardener.*

Cathedral Glass
Machine rolled transparent colored glass.

Cats Paw
Opalescent glass with a mottled appearance that suggests cat paw prints.

Caulking
Material used to waterproof and hold a window in place.

Cementing
Forcing a putty compound between the glass and the metal flange to add strength and make the window waterproof.

Centigrade
A scale used for recording temperature at which water freezes at 0° C and boils at 100° C.

Ceramic Fiber Insulation

Light weight alumina silicate fibers used in kiln construction that absorb less heat—making the kiln more economical.

Cerium Oxide

A powder mixed into a slurry that is used in polishing glass.

C.F.M.

Cubic feet per minute. Used in the measurement of air movement.

Chain Loop

The ring on the top of a hanging lamp to which a chain connects.

Chair

A wooden bench or chair with arms at which the gaffer fashions an object.

Chamber, (Annealing)

That part of the kiln used to cool down fired glass.

Chancel

The east portion of the church set aside for the clergy and choir.

Channel

'U' shaped groove in the came in which the glass sits.

Channel Depth

Measurement from the top to the bottom of the channel.

Channel Glazing

A method of glazing which uses removable surface mounted 'U' shapes.

Channel Width

Measurement of the inside of the channel.

Charge

The loading of the batch in the furnace.

Check

A surface crack. An imperfection.

Chemical Durability

The ability to withstand wear and decay from exposure to corrosive materials. Glass ranks high in chemical durability.

Chiaroscuro

Technique of artistic representation that makes use of obviously contrasting lights and darks, especially to create the illusion of space and volume (used mainly in painting).

Chill Mark

A wrinkled surface on glass resulting from uneven cooling in the forming process.

Chipped Glass

A technique where glue pulls the surface of the glass causing it to chip. See *Glue Chip*.

Chuck

A device to hold a tool in a lathe or drill.

Cinquefoil

1. A small opening in Gothic tracery having five arcs. 2. A garland having five loops.

Circle Cutter

A glass cutter with a pivoting arm used to cut circles out of glass.

Clear Acid

Hydrofluoric acid which gives a clear etch and eats down through the surface of the glass. (See *Hydrofluoric acid*)

Clerestory

The upper part of the nave above the side aisles of a church.

Cloisonné

A technique using wires shaped into a design and secured to a metal base which is filled with enamels, fired, ground and polished.

Close Millefiori

Tightly packed random arrangement of millefiori canes.

Cloudy Glass

Cathedral glass mixed with white opalescent glass resembling clouds. See *Wispy*.

Coating Cement

A material used to coat fiber molds and kiln floors, protects in the event of a glass melt down.

Coefficient of Expansion

The number indicating the percentage of change in length per degree centigrade change in temperature. Important in fusing glass.

C.O.H.

Center for Occupational Hazards.

Cohesion

The state or act of sticking together.

Cold End

The discharge end of a lehr.

Cold Joint

Solder that is melted but not actually attached firmly to both pieces of metal.

Collage

A design made of bits of glass and other materials glued to a background.

Colloidal Colors

Colors which are due to the presence of a pigment in an extremely finely divided or colloidal state. Gold ruby colors in both glass and paints are examples. Extended heating will cause the colloidal particles to grow, shifting the color, in the case of gold rubies, more to the blue, becoming more purplish. See *Striking*.

Coloring

Selecting the colors of glass for a window.

Color Intensity

The degree of purity or brilliance of a color.

Color Pigments

Ground coloring materials supported in a thick liquid.

Color Selection

The very careful choice of colored glass, under natural light, so that an exact choice or replacement is possible. In restoration work a large inventory or 'library' is essential so that when pieces are replaced, the selection is not constrained or limited. Literally thousands of colors, textures, and densities are possible.

Color Value

The relationship of a color to lightness or darkness.

Combing

Dragging or pulling a sharp instrument through multi-colored molten glass to achieve a feathery effect.

Commercial Glass

Clear heavy glass with a pattern pressed on one side.

Compatible

Different glasses which have the same, or very close, co-efficient of expansion; therefore, they can be fused together without undue stress.

Complementary Colors

Colors which appear opposite each other on the color wheel. When mixed together, they neutralize each other.

Complex Curve

A curve that bends in several different directions such as a sphere.

Composition

The overall design of a finished piece containing balance of color and linear flow.

Compound

A formulation of ingredients producing a polymer, pigmented filler used for caulking.

Compressor

A pump and pressure tank used to supply air under pressure for abrasive etching.

Concave Bead

Bead of glazing compound with a concave exposed surface.

Conchoidal

Having elevations or depressions in form like one half of a bi-valve shell.

Cone

Elongated triangle ceramic form that sags or bends at a specific temperature, used to indicate heat penetration during firing of a kiln. See *Pyrometric Cone.*

Confetti Glass

Thin chips of various colored glass applied to one side of the glass during manufacture.(See *Fractured Glass, Stringer Glass*)

Consistency

The degree of softness or hardness of a compound.

Consultation Agreement

Arrangements between the States and O.S.H.A. to establish state services available at no cost to employers and assist them in establishing effective occupational safety and health programs.

Continuous Furnace

A furnace operated on an uninterrupted cycle. The charge is constantly added.

Convex Bead

Bead of glazing compound with a convex exposed surface.

Cool Colors

Blue, green, and variants.

Copper Foil

1. The mil-thickness copper material, often adhesive backed, used to join separate pieces of glass. 2. The technique of joining pieces of glass where foil is centered on the edge of each glass piece, then bent over the edge to cover a very small portion of the back and front faces of the glass. Pieces are abutted and solder is melted over the exposed foil surfaces, causing the foil covered glass edges to become joined.

Copper Patina

A chemical solution used to produce a copper color on a soldered surface.

Copper Wheel Engraving

Glass engraving using finely shaped copper wheels and an abrasive spinning on a lathe to cut designs into glass.

Cords

Optical distortions, similar to waves, that appear in glass.

Cork Wheel

The third stage of the beveling process. A large, vertically mounted cork covered wheel and a pumice slurry produces a dull semi-opaque finish.

Corrosion

The process of being worn or eaten away through oxidation.

Counter Enameling

Applying enamel on both sides of a piece.

Crackel (craquel) Glass

Antique glass with cracked texture which has been intentionally introduced during the cooling process.

Crazing

Tiny random cracks on the surface of the glass.

Crosshatch

Lines in one direction crossed by lines in another direction.

Crown

Glass above the motif. (See *Dome*)

Crown Glass

A circular platter of glass formed by spinning molten glass at the end of a pontil, with a pontil mark in the center. See *Rondel, Roundel.*

Crucible

A ceramic pot in which glass in melted.

Cruciform

Cross shaped.

Crystal Glass

Glass of exceptional clarity and brilliance.

Cullet

Scraps of broken or waste glass that make up a new glass batch, as opposed to using raw ingredients.

Cupping

Method for forming brushes by placing bundles of hair, point downward, into a metal cup, the inside of which has the same shape as the brush desired.

Cure

The transformation of the resin from the liquid to the stable solid state.

Curious Glass

Glass made on a trial basis, usually one of a kind.

Cusp

The projecting points formed by the intersection of two segmental arcs or foils.

Cut Glass

Glass decorated by the use of cutting wheels with abrasives. The glass is polished, giving it a brilliant appearance.

Cutline

A full-sized drawing of the exact configuration and specification to which leaded glass is to be cut.

Cutting Glass

Glass is not 'cut'—it is scored, producing a scratch, or score line in the glass surface, that, with pressure will cause a fracture along the score line. Glass may also be cut with abrasive diamond saws or abrasive water jets. (See *Fracture, Score*)

Cylinder

A glass shape formed during antique glass production, prior to being cut and flattened. See *Cannon, Muff.*

D.A.

Machine drawn antique glass. See *Semi-Antique.*

Dalle de Verre

A thick slab of cast stained glass that is cut or broken and cemented into a panel with an epoxy adhesive matrix. See *Faceted Glass* or *Slab Glass.*

Dap

A commercial name of a caulking or cementing compound.

Daylight

Visible opening size.

Day Tank

A tank in which a batch of glass is melted overnight for the next day's work.

Decalcomania

Designs printed in ceramic colors on special decal paper which can be transferred from the paper to glass or ceramic and then fired to the proper maturing temperature for the paint. See *Decal Paper.*

Decal Paper

A special heavy stock paper on which is printed an even coating of a water soluble gum, such as dextrin. A ceramic design is printed on this paper, and then covercoated with a clear lacquer. When the paper is immersed in water, the gum dissolves and the design, held together now by the clear lacquer, slides off and is placed on the glass or ceramic on which it will be fired.

Deep Cut

Depth of cut in carving or sand-blasting glass or other material.

Deer Foot

A special brush shape used for stippling which is cylindrical with a bottom surface that is tilted from the horizontal.

Design

1. A composition, arrangement, or pattern. 2. A scale drawing of a stained glass window used for color selection.

Detergent Resistant

Withstands the action of alkaline solutions, such as detergents. See *Alkali Resistant.*

Devitrification

Crystallization in glass occurring as scum on the surface of the glass.

Diamond Point Engraving

Hand engraving of glass using a diamond tipped instrument or scribe.

Diapering

A glass painting technique that makes use of very decorative designs containing repetitive floral patterns, small squares or lozenges.

Dichroic Glass

Space-age application of super thin, clear layers of metal oxides which allows for either transmitted or reflected color, depending on the viewer's viewing position.

Die-Cut Stencil

Vinyl-based stencil material incised by a photo-etched plate (die) used to eliminate hand cutting.

Direct Emulsion Screen

A screen coated with a photosensitive emulsion on which a pattern is exposed and developed and used as a stencil.

Displacement C.F.M.

A measure of a compressor's ability to deliver air (cubic feet per minute.)

Dividing Iron

Medieval tool. The tip was heated to crack glass.

Dog Tooth

Ornamental motif consisting of raised pyramids.

Dome

Glass above the motif. See *Crown.*

Double Glazing

The use of two pieces of glass, one in front of the other, with an air space between for insulation.

Double Hung

A window consisting of two sashes of glass operating in a rectangular frame. Both upper and lower halves slide up and down to open.

Double Strength Glass

One-eighth inch thick glass. Strength refers to thickness.

Down-draw

The process of continuously drawing glass downward from an orifice.

Draft

The slight angle on the side of a mold to allow the casting to be removed.

Drag Ladle

Gathering molten glass from the furnace and dropping it in water to produce frit.

Drapery

The painting on glass that defines the drapery robes of figures, usually Biblical.

Drapery Glass

Heavily manipulated, folded or rippled glass that forms 'drapes' that may be one inch or more thick.

Drawn Glass

Glass formed by vertical pulling. (See *Fourcault Method*)

Dross

Impurities found in solder.

Dry Glazing

A method of securing glass in a frame with just resilient gaskets.

Dry Strength

The strength a material acquires after it dries, but before it is fired (primarily referring to clay molds.)

Duplication Mold

A mold made by casting over another article.

Dura Board

A spun alumina silicate fiber ideal for high firing to 2200 °F.

Duranoidic

A process producing a bronze finish on anodized aluminum.

Durometer

An instrument used in rating hardness.

Dust Collector

Equipment used to collect dust from sandblasting.

Dutchman

To cover a crack during repair, a flange of lead is applied over the crack, tucked under adjoining leads and soldered in place. This procedure has generally been replaced with either edge gluing or a thin copper foiled line.

Early English

The classic phase of English Gothic in the thirteenth century characteristic of tall narrow lancet style windows.

Earth Colors

Pigments such as yellow ochre and umber that are obtained by mining.

Easel

An upright glass plate on which glass pieces are applied with wax or plasticine and viewed for color selection, or to assist with determining the amount of light to be controlled by the application of paint.

East End

The east or altar end of the church. The area is not necessarily compass east.

Edge Clearance

The distance between the edge of a unit of glass and the frame.

Edge Work

Refers to grinding, sanding, or polishing the edge of the glass.

Edging Line

Bank of glass sometimes with painted designs, placed as an edging around a panel. See *Border, Fillet.*

Elasticity

The capacity to return to the initial form or state following deformation.

Electrode

Either terminal of an electric source.

Electrolyte

A material that aids in the suspension of enamel in a clay enamel mixture.

Element (electrical)

A coil of resistance wire through which electrical current passes, creating heat in a kiln.

Embossed

Having a raised, decorative design.

Embossing Black

Black acid resistant paint.

Emery

A granular mineral substance used for grinding and polishing.

Emery Cloth

Fine grained abrasive material used for sanding.

Employee Training

O.S.H.A. programs required by both the Lead Standard and the Hazard Communication Program. See *Training Program.*

Emulsion

The light sensitive/light hardening material used to make photo stencils on a silkscreen.

Enamel

Pigment applied to the surface of the glass and fired, thus coating the surface of the glass with color, either transparent or opaque. Usually refers to transparent, low fire colors. See *Vitreous Paint.*

End of Day

Usually refers to one-of-a-kind items that glass blowers are free to make on their own from the vat's leftovers after the day's production is done.

Endomosaic

Combination of stained glass and mosaic.

English Stippler

Round four-inch long horse or hog hair brush used for stippling matted paint on glass.

Engraver

An electric tool used to cut into the glass surface.

Engraving

1. Cutting into the surface of the glass. 2. A design using diamond or copper wheel techniques.

Epoxy

A plastic cement made up of resin mixed with a hardener.

Essence

A volatile liquid for thinning metallic paints.

Etching

The surface erosion of glass by chemical or mechanical means.

European Antique

Mouth blown antique glass from Europe and England.

Eutectic

The lowest melting point of a given mixture.

Exhaust Fan

A fan in the sandblast booth creating an air flow to remove the dust.

Exhaust System

A ventilating system to remove dust from a sandblast booth, painting area or work area.

Exotherm

The heat given off from the action of the catalyst on the resin.

Exposure Monitoring

Testing and determination to discover if any employee is exposed to lead at or above the action level.

Exterior Glazed

Glass set from the exterior of the building.

Exterior Stop

The molding that holds the light on the exterior of the frame.

Eye

The hottest part of the furnace.

Fabricut

An open weave cloth used to sand the separator from a kiln shelf.

Facade

The front of a building.

Face Glazing

The triangle bead of caulk that serves as the outside stop when glazing a window with only one stop. See *Front Putty*.

Faceted Glass

Stained glass windows made of Dalle glass and a matrix. See *Dalle de Verre, Slab Glass*.

Faceting

Chipping the edge of dalles, knocking off a concentric half circle chip of glass.

Facing

The finished surface of caulking on a window.

Fahrenheit

The temperature scale commonly used in the United States, at which water freezes at 32° F and boils at 212° F.

Favrile

Iridescent glass patented by Louis Comfort Tiffany in the 1880s, produced by the exposure of hot glass to metallic fumes and oxides.

Felt Wheel

The final stage of the beveling process. A felt surface wheel charged with cerium oxide polishes the glass to a brilliant and clear finish.

Fenestration

The arrangement of windows in a structure.

Ferrule

The tube, usually either metal or quill, into which the hair bundle of a brush is fitted to secure it to the handle.

Fiberglass

A material made from strands of glass.

Fiber Paper

A thin, ceramic fiber material which does not stick to glass at high temperature, for use in bas relief or to cover a kiln shelf.

Fid

A small, often conically shaped wooden hand tool used to open lead flanges prior to glazing. See *Lathekin*.

Field

The design area used as a background between medallions.

Figured Glass

Flat glass having a pattern on one or both surfaces.

Filigree

Transparent glass that has colored threads in it.

Fillers

Material added to expand the volume of other materials.

Fillet

A thin strip, or border of glass.

Fine

To melt glass until it is free of bubbles.

Fined

A glass melt that is without bubbles.

Finial
The knob that goes on top of a lamp harp, or, architecturally, an ornament that caps a feature of a building.

Firebrick
Soft porous brick that withstands high temperatures used for lining kilns.

Fire Over
To let the furnace soak at working temperature.

Fire Polishing
Polishing glass by heating to the point the surface remelts, leaving it smooth.

Fire Scale
Scaling of metals in a kiln due to repeated firings.

Firing
The heating of glass in a kiln.

Firing Down
The addition of a small amount of heat to the kiln while cooling through the annealing range to cool more slowly.

Firing Schedule
The record of time and temperature during the fusing cycle.

Firing Temperature
Temperature to which a paint must be raised in order to allow it to melt and fuse to the surface on which it has been applied. See *Maturing Temperature.*

Fissure
See *Score.*

Fitch Hair
A European weasel's hair, which is fairly stiff and springy, and is frequently used to make excellent stippling brushes.

Fixative
Spray used on drawings to make them more permanent.

Fixed Window
A window permanently fastened to the frame.

Flamboyant
Fifteenth century French Gothic style, characterized by flame like forms.

Flameware
Pyrex type glass that will take direct heat and not thermal crack.

Flange
The sides of lead came. See *Leaf.*

Flanging
Soldering on an extra piece of lead to cover thick pieces of glass.

Flash
A thin coating of colored glass applied to a base glass.

Flashed Glass
Sheet glass, usually clear, with a thin layer of colored glass on one side.

Flemish Glass
Clear cathedral glass with a large wavelike pattern on both sides.

Flexible Shaft
A long rotating shaft attached to a motor so the rotating tool is used away from the motor.

Flint Glass
A term for any clear glass except low expansion borosilicates, such as pyrex.

Flints
Planned breaks in a diamond or rectangular window to break up the geometric design.

Float Plate Glass
Flat glass manufactured by floating the ribbon of drawn, molten glass on a long bath of molten tin, and fire-polishing the upper surface, yielding a smooth polished surface on both sides.

Floret
See *Cane.*

Flow Point
The temperature at which heated solder liquifies.

Fluting
A pattern of deep narrow grooves.

Flux
A substance that promotes fusion. 1. A chemical agent that removes oxidation allowing soldering to take place. 2. Colorless low melt glass powder that carries pigment into the glass. 3. A substance used in the glass batch to facilitate fusion. 4. Colorless low melting glass powder which is milled with pigments to produce glass paints.

F.N.A.
French new antique glass, a machine drawn antique glass. See *Semi-antique.*

Foil
See *Copper Foil.*

Foiling
The process of covering the glass edge with copper foil.

Forming
The shaping or molding of hot glass.

Fourcault Method
A vertical drawn method of glass making.

Fractured Glass
(See *Confetti Glass, Stringer Glass*)

Fracture
To break or crack the glass on the score line. (See *Score, Score Line*)

Fragmentation
Sections or shards of glass fired together.

Free Blown
Glass blown in the air without a mold. See *Off Hand.*

French Chalk
A preparation of powdered talc used for marking on glass.

French Embossing
A system of etching with two or more acids. The procedure leaves a multilevel, multi tone etching.

Frigger

An experimental or apprentice piece.

Frit

Crushed, ground or thermal shocked glass varying in size from powders to small chunks.

Frit Mill

A crushing tool used to break up glass into frit.

Fritting

The rapid chilling of the molten glass by quenching it in water to produce frit.

Front Putty

The putty forming the triangular fillet serving as the outside stop on a window. See *Face Glazing*.

Frosted Glass

Glass with a white translucent surface resulting from sandblasting or etching.

Frying

Tiny holes or cracking in glass paint because of too high a firing temperature, too thick a coat of paint, or the addition of too much gum.

F.S.A.

French semi-antique, a machine drawn antique glass. See *also F.N.A.*

Full Antique

Mouth blown antique sheet glass.

Full Size

The outside dimension of a panel. Also, the full scale cartoon.

Fuming

Coating the surface of glass with a metallic spray for a iridescent surface.

Fuse

To liquefy by means of heat. To melt and unite.

Fused Glass

Combining glass pieces by melting them together.

Fuse to Stick

Fusing only hot enough so the pieces of glass stick together but do not blend or melt into one. See *Tack Fuse*.

Gaffer

The master craftsman in charge of a shop of off hand glass blowers.

Galvanic Action

Electrolytic action between two different metals that has a degenerative effect on the metals.

Gamboge

Yellow pigment, and ingredient of silver stain.

Garnet

Hard glass-like minerals used as an abrasive.

G.A.S.

Glass Art Society.

Gasket

Material used to seal a joint.

Gather

The glob of glass collected from the furnace on the end of the blowpipe or punty.

Gatherer

The craftsman who takes the gather of molten glass from the furnace and starts to blow the form.

Gauge

A measurement to indicate thickness.

Gel

The state of the resin prior to its becoming a hard solid.

Gelatin Sheet

A transparent gelatin film used in making photographic screen stencils.

Gemmaux

A process whereby small pieces of colored glass are glued and then grouted to an underlying piece of clear window glass to form a pattern.

Gilding

Applying a thin layer of gold or silver metallic paint to a surface.

Glass

A hard brittle substance, usually transparent, formed by fusing silica, alkali, and other chemicals.

Glass Bending

Sagging or draping glass over a mold by heating in a kiln. See *Slumping*.

Glass Blowing

The process of shaping an object from molten glass by blowing air into it through a tube, or blowpipe.

Glass Cutter

A hand held tool with a cutting wheel used for scoring glass prior to separating it.

Glass Cylinder

Hand blown large cylinder bubble that is cut and laid flat into a sheet. See *Antique Glass, Cannon, Muff*.

Glass Decorator

Anyone that alters a glass article after its initial manufacture.

Glass Etch

Any of several compounds that permit the frosting of glass.

Glass Globs

Thick round pieces of stained glass, from ½″ to 2″ in diameter.

Glass House

The factory where glass is made.

Glass Jewels

Small pieces of clear or colored glass that have been faceted, molded or domed.

Glass Lathe

A small bench mounted machine used for engraving designs on glass.

Glass Maker's Soap

Black oxide of manganese which added to the batch, neutralizes the natural color of the metallic impurities such as iron.

Glass Paint

Vitreous paints composed of metallic oxides and ground glass in a liquid vehicle then fired on glass. See *Enamels, Glass Stainers Paints.*

Glass Size Line

The perimeter line of the panel.

Glass Stainer Paints

Vitreous paints, usually blacks, browns and flesh reds, used primarily for tracing and matting; fired at about 1,200° F, they are weather resistant and very opaque. See *Weather Resistant Colors.*

Glaze

A thin vitreous coating that gives a gloss or smoothness to the glass.

Glazier

A person who installs glass in window frames. Also, the person who assembles the pieces of glass and lead to make a window.

Glazing

The process of assembling pieces of glass and lead to make a window.

Glazing Knife

Knife used to cut lead came when making a stained glass panel. See *Lead Knife.*

Glazing Laws

Federal, state, and local laws that regulate certain types of flat glass installed in hazardous or potentially hazardous situations.

Globe

A large glass ball that fits over the light bulb to diffuse its light.

Globe Holder

A brass ring that holds the globe.

Glory Hole

The small furnace used to quickly reheat glass while it is being hand worked.

Glue Chip

The application of heated animal glue to sandblasted glass that when dry, chips off leaving a crystalline or icy look.

Gob

A portion of molten glass delivered to a mold for forming.

Goethe Glass

A clear blown glass without seeds or striation, just a slight surface distortion from the blowing process, similar to old window glass.

Gold Stone

A gold aventurine glass.

Gothic

A style, generally referring to architecture, found in western Europe from 12th through 16th centuries.

G.N.A.

German new antique, a machine drawn antique glass. Also called *D.A.*

Grain

Indicates the size of an abrasive particle. The number indicates the number of openings in a wire mesh in one inch.

Granite Back Glass

Cathedral glass with a rolled bumpy, rough texture on one surface of the glass.

Graphic Process

A stencil made by a photographic process used for sandblasting or painting.

Gray

In glass color, an addition of nickel or other metallic oxides to dull the color when the glass is made.

Green Glass

The natural color of glass, the result of impurities in the batch.

Greenware

A molded clay object that is just dried or partially fired.

Grid Cutting

A set of shallow, narrow grooves cut in glass.

Grinding

The removal of glass by abrasive action.

Grisaille

A panel or window of clear or light colored glass painted with geometric or foliate designs. Sometimes used to refer to glass paints.

Grit

Very fine abrasive particles, usually dust size

Grizzling

The decomposition of the glass. It has a dull look, the result of very fine pitting as the glass disintegrates.

Grog

Clay that has been fired and ground. It is added to clay to reduce shrinkage.

Grout

A mortar or putty used to fill in the space between the lead and the glass pieces, providing weather proofing and stability. See *Putty.*

Groze

To bite or chip unwanted edges from a piece of glass using a grozing plier.

Grozing Iron

A flat iron bar with notches on its edge used to chip and shape the glass edge.

Grozing Pliers

Flat nosed plier with the temper removed, used to chip away small amounts of glass from the edge.

Gum Arabic

The powdered gum of the acacia tree which acts as a binder for water mixed paints.

Hake Brush
A bamboo handled natural fiber brush from the Orient with absorbent and retentive qualities.

Halation
A phenomenon where light colored glass, when surrounded by darker glass, seems to spread beyond actual boundaries, creating a halo effect.

Halftone
1. In silkscreening, a film positive made from a photograph in which all gray tones have been translated into black dots of varying density. 2. In glass painting, a line or area that has shades of tone from translucent to opaque.

Hammered Glass
Cathedral glass with a tiny tight uniform pattern of round smooth knobs.

Hand Engraved
All engraving which requires hand manipulation of the engraver or the glass.

Hardener
A catalyst that causes thermoplastic resins to harden.

Harp
The brass fitting on a lamp base that fits around the bulb to hold the lamp shade.

Hazard Communication
An O.S.H.A. program requiring that information about all hazards associated with any and all chemicals used within the United States be transmitted to employers and employees. See *O.S.H.A.*

Hazard Evaluation
The review of scientific evidence regarding hazards associated with chemicals.

Hazardous Material
A material with the potential to cause adverse health effects or to pose physical hazards, such as flammability. See *Toxic Material.*

H Bar
An 'H' shaped metal bar used as a support between two sections of a panel.

Heart
The center, or core, of lead came that connects the two flanges, or leaves.

Heat Soak
To maintain a specific kiln temperature for a given time; i.e., to aid annealing.

Heat Transfer
The movement of heat from a warmer to a cooler body by convection, conduction, or radiation.

Heel Ball
Black wax used to make rubbings of glass panels during restoration.

H.E.P.A. Filter
High Efficiency Particulate Filter. This filter is capable of removing essentially all solid particles from air passed through it.

High Heart Lead
Came with a long cross bar on the lead that sometimes has a heavier top leaf. Can be used in plating or with thick glass.

Hopper
A window whose sash is hinged at the bottom.

Horizontal Slider
A window where the moveable panel slides horizontally.

Hot Glass
Glass that is worked in the molten state. See *Blown Glass, Free Blown, Off Hand.*

Hue
The light tint of color in clear glass. Also another word for color.

Hydrocal
A high-fire plaster, when mixed with silica flour makes a mold with fine detail, used often in pate de verre or lost wax castings.

Hydrofluoric Acid
The only material that attacks silica, the basic ingredient of glass. It is used for etching glass, is considered hazardous, and must be used with caution.

I.A.R.C.
International Agency for Research on Cancer.

Ice
Granular enamel paint which will give a pebbled or crinkled appearance when fired on the glass.

Iconography
A comprehensive plan for the subjects of works of art, not necessarily Christian.

Inactive
The part of a window that is non-movable.

Incandescence
The emission of visible light by a hot object.

Incise
To engrave or cut.

Inclusion
Any bubble or foreign matter enclosed in the glass.

Indirect Screen
A screen to which a photosensitive film is attached in order to form a stencil.

Infinite Switch
A type of temperature control with multiple settings.

Infrared
Rays of light with a wave length longer than those of visible light at the red end of the spectrum.

Ingestion
To take lead or other toxic elements into your system by eating or drinking.

Inhalation
To take lead or other toxic elements into your lungs by breathing.

Initial Heat

The first stage in the heating cycle up to the strain point.

Inside Casing

Wooden interior framing of a window.

In Situ

In position.

Insulation Brick

Heat resistant soft porous brick.

Intaglio

Deep cut engraved design either cut or pressed into the glass.

Interior Glazed

Glass set from the interior of the building.

Ionic Migration

The movement of silver ions into the glass matrix to replace sodium and potassium ions and stain the glass yellow. See *Silver Stain*.

Iridescence

A surface treatment on glass that has a shiny mother-of-pearl look.

Iridizing Solution

Metallic salt dissolved in hydrochloric solution that contains chlorides or nitrates and tin, iron, bismuth, and antimony.

Isothermal glazing

System of protective outer glazing that inhibits conductivity of heat from the exterior to the interior surface of the complete window unit.

Isotropic

Refers to materials whose properties are the same throughout, such as glass.

Jack

A spring tool used to work molten glass.

Jamb

The upright surface forming the side of a window.

Jar Mill

A porcelain jar revolving on its axis containing a charge of flint pebbles or porcelain balls, used to reduce colors and other ceramic materials to a fine powder or slurry. See *Ball Mill*.

J Channel

A 'J' shaped aluminum channel.

Jewel

See *Glass Jewel*

Jig

1. A guide or template to hold or direct a tool. Generally used for the production of identical multiple components. 2. A stabilizing device.

Joint

See *Lead Joint*.

Juxtaposition

Two or more elements in close spatial relationship.

Kaolin

China clay, a major component of shelf primer.

Kiln

A high temperature insulated oven used for firing glass.

Kiln Furniture

Ceramic spacers used to support the kiln shelves.

Kiln Sitter

A mechanical device using a pyrometric cone to shut off the kiln.

Kiln Wash

A refractory powder mixed with water used as a coating to keep the glass from the shelf. See *Alumina Hydrate, Separator, Shelf Primer*.

Knapping

A side tap on a glass dalle that chips off a piece of glass making the facet.

Labels and Labeling

Identity markers required by O.S.H.A. to be placed on all hazardous chemicals, also listing hazard warnings and information about the manufacturer.

Laminate

Glass constructed in successive layers that is glued or tack fired.

Laminated Safety Glass

Two sheets of clear glass bonded together with a sheet of clear plastic in the middle.

Lamp Jig

An adjustable form that allows a lampshade under construction to be turned to maintain a horizontal attitude for soldering.

Lampblack

A fine black carbon powder used to darken cement and putty used to caulk stained glass panels.

Lampwork

The working and shaping of glass over a gas burner or torch.

Lancet

A long narrow window with a pointed arch.

Lantern

A tower, usually in the center or crossing of a church, with windows to admit light into the interior.

Lathe

A machine that holds and turns work while being worked with a tool.

Lathekin

1. A small wood or hard plastic tool used to open or manipulate lead came. 2. A burnishing tool for use with copper foil.

Lavender Oil

A light essential oil used as a painting medium for enamels.

Lead Burden

See *Total Body Burden*.

Lead Came
Extruded lead channel with a H or U cross section to hold the glass in the panel. See *Came*.

Lead Crystal
A clear, brilliant glass containing at least 24% lead, generally lead oxide, by weight.

Lead Knife
See *Glazing Knife*.

Leaded Glass
Windows or panels in which the glass pieces are bound together with lead cames. See *Stained Glass*.

Leading
1. Assembling a work of stained glass where metal came is the binding material. 2. The matrix of came strips of a leaded glass window.

Leading Up
The process of joining pieces of glass in a stained glass panel by means of lead.

Lead Joint
The intersection of two or more lead cames.

Lead Line
A line produced on a full-size drawing of a leaded window to indicate the position of the lead came.

Lead Poisoning
A diseased condition resulting from the bio-absorption of lead into the human system. See *Plumbism*.

Lead Release
The process of bio-availability of lead caused by leaching of fired paints and glazes on ceramic ware and lead crystal glass as a result of contact with food acids.

Lead Standard
A U.S. Federal law regarding worker exposure to lead. It is under administered by O.S.H.A.

Lead Vise
A mechanism that holds one end of the lead while the other end is pulled to stretch the lead for strength.

Leaf
The component of lead came that fits over the glass. See *Flange*.

Lehr (Lear—Lier)
A long tunnel shaped oven used to anneal, or cool, glass under controlled conditions.

Lens Cutter
A mechanical glass cutter capable of cutting only small circles.

Light
An opening through which sunlight is admitted, also a section of a large window, usually found in series divided by mullions.

Light Table
A box or table, lit from below and topped with diffusing glass, generally used to trace patterns, check glass colors and facilitate painting.

Linear
Composed of lines.

Liner
A thin brush used to make lines or stripes.

Liquidus Temperature
The temperature at which devitrification forms.

Liver of Sulfur
A sulfur compound, called patina, for darkening metal.

Low Expansion Colors
Colors having a lower coefficient of expansion which will be compatible with low expansion glasses.

Luster
A varnish-like solution of metallic resinates in essential oils which, when fired on glass, will give brilliant iridescent or metallic films.

Luster Essence
A mixture of essential oils and solvents used to thin or extend lusters.

Machine Guards
Methods or barriers designed to protect the operator and/or others in the machine operation area from hazards associated with the machine or process.

Mahl Stick (Maul)
A stick used by painters as a rest for the hand while working.

Malleable
Easily shaped by means of pressure.

Maquette
A small scale preliminary model of proposed work.

Marbling
Method of getting random pattern on glass, either with paint or stopping out agent prior to aciding.

Marinite
A heavy duty refractory board used as a kiln shelf.

Marver (Marvel)
The flat steel table on which molten glass is rolled and shaped.

Marvering
The act of rolling molten glass on the steel table.

Mastic
Adhesive that remains pliable with age.

Material Safety Data Sheet
A listing of information about a single chemical material, including information on hazardous characteristics, health and safety information, precautions for safe handling and emergency first aid procedures. (*M.S.D.S.*)

Matrix
Opaque material used as a cement to hold the glass in place in a faceted panel.

Matt
A dull finish vitreous paint laid evenly over the glass surface that must be fired.

Matting

The application of a thin slurry of vitreous paint over a wide area of glass prior to blending.

Mature

The desired fired state of glass—neither over nor under fired.

Maturing Temperature

Temperature to which a paint must be raised in order to allow it to melt to fuse with the substrate surface on which it has been applied. See *Firing Temperature*.

Maul Stick

See *Mahl Stick*.

Medallion

A small, bordered picture area of a window, primarily of the twelfth and thirteenth centuries.

Medallion Window

A window (generally Medieval) comprised of repeated geometric enclosure devices often depicting different biblical scenes.

Medical Removal

Temporary removal of an employee from work in a contaminated area due of elevated retention of toxic materials, or other health conditions. Return is dependent a medically measured decrease in toxicity to a mandated lower level.

Medieval

A time period that included the Romanesque and Gothic periods, also called 'The Middle Ages,' from about A.D. 500 to 1500.

Medium

1. The material used for an art expression. 2. The liquid used with glass paints.

Mending Lead

Thin lead, also called a *dutchman,* used to support a crack.

Mercury Oxide Yellow

Often previously used to dilute burnished gold.

Mesh Count

The number of holes per linear inch in a fabric or screen. The higher the count, the finer the definition of the print, and the thinner the deposit of paint on the substrate.

Metal

1. A term used by glassmakers for glass. 2. A term used by glaziers to refer to the leading matrix.

Metaling

A condition that occurs from either over-firing silver stain or from too heavy an application of stain, which leaves an opaque residue on the glass.

Metallic Lusters

Gilding paints in noble metals, such as gold, silver, palladium and platinum, and others.

Metallic Overglaze

Firing very fine metal particles onto the glass resulting in a shiny metallic surface.

Metallic Oxides

Metals combined with oxygen used as enamel and glass colorants.

Mica

A mineral silicate that when laminated between glass being fused will create bubbles.

Millefiori

Bundles of glass canes fused together into a rod, frequently in a floral pattern. See *Cane*.

Mineral Spirits

A solvent and cleaner.

Miter Cut

A cut at an angle other than 90°.

Mohs' Scale

A scale of relative mineral hardness.

Moil

Glass remaining on the pontil after the piece is complete.

Moisture Trap

Filter used to trap oil and water emitted as mist and/or vapor from a working air compressor.

Mold

1. A form used to shape glass in the slumping process. 2. A form on which a lampshade is constructed.

Mold Blown Glass

Glass blown into a rigid wood or metal form.

Mold Release

A substance used to coat the mold to prevent sticking.

Molecule

A unit of matter, the smallest portion of an element or compound that retains chemical identity with the substance in mass.

Molten

Made liquid by heat.

Monel Metal

A nickel-copper alloy that resists fire scale formation.

Mono-lastic

A type of caulking.

Monomer

A reactive material used with resin that makes the resin less viscous and easier to handle.

Mop

A brush used to apply a wet, thin, translucent paint wash.

Mosaic

1. A design made by setting tessera of glass, wood, stone or other materials in a matrix. 2. Leaded glass windows comprised of many small pieces.

Motif

A design or decoration.

Mouth Blown

Glass produced by forcing air, by mouth, through a blowpipe into molten glass. See *Antique Glass*.

M.S.D.S.
See *Material Safety Data Sheet.*

Muff
See *Glass Cylinder.*

Muffle
An enclosed furnace in which glass is heated without exposing it directly to fire.

Muller
A flat bottomed glass pestle for grinding paint powder on a glass palette.

Mullion
The vertical strip dividing the panes of a window.

Mullite
A high alumina material used for kiln shelves.

Multilevel
The different elevations of cutting, etching or engraving to obtain bas relief.

Muntin
A horizontal strip dividing panes of a window.

Murano
An island near Venice. The traditional home of famous glass factories.

Mushroom
In stained glass, the emergence of cement in a mushroom shape between two pieces of glass.

Narthex
The vestibule, or entrance of a church.

Nave
The long central portion of a church auditorium.

Negative
The reverse or opposite.

Negative Painting
A reverse glass painting technique done on the back side of glass in which the detail is painted before the background. Usually done with unfired paints.

Negative Printing
A process of using fired glass paints where the background is matted to form an opaque base from which the letters are scratched out prior to firing.

Negative Space
Any part of a glass window through which no light is transmitted, usually the dark lead line, matrix area of a window, and/or an opaque painted area.

Neo Gothic
Nineteenth Century revival of Gothic style.

Nichrome
A refractory alloy of nickel, iron, and chromium that is not subject to fire scale.

N.I.O.S.H.
National Institute of Occupational Safety and Health.

Nip
To bite or chip away the edge of the glass.

Nippers
Special dikes or cutters used to cut lead came.

Nipples
Threaded rod used to hold lampshade to lamp base.

Nondrying
A compound that does not form a surface skin after application, or is not subject to evaporation.

Nonrepresentational
Not representing any object. Not realistic.

Norman Slabs
Glass blown into a rectangular mold and cut apart on the corners, resulting in square or rectangular pieces that are thin at the edges and thick in the middle.

North Side
The north or left side of a church is traditionally the side of darkness and the Old Testament, which is often reflected in the subject matter and colors of these windows. It is not necessarily compass north.

Nozzle
A tapered spout at the end of the sandblast hose.

N.T.P.
National Toxicology Program.

Oaktag
Pale amber colored 90 lb.-weight paper used in pattern making.

Obscure
Non-transparent glass resulting from painting, sandblasting or acid etching.

Oculus
A circular window without stone tracery. Also called Occhio, Occhi, Oculu.

Off Hand
Blowing and forming glass without a mold. See *Free Blown.*

Ogee
A continuous S shaped reverse curve.

Oil Cutter
A glass cutter that has an oil reservoir in the handle.

Oil of Spike
Solvent for enamel medium.

Opak
White opal flash on a colored antique.

Opalescent Glass
Non-transparent or semi-opaque machine rolled glass often with two or more colors streaked together. See *Opal Glass.*

Opal Glass
A glass with a milky or resinous appearance. See *Opalescent Glass.*

Opaque
Not transparent.

Opaque Enamels
Glass enamels that are not transparent.

Opus Sectile

Opaque glass mosaic, cut into shapes and sometimes painted and fired.

O.S.H.A.

Occupational Safety and Health Administration, charged with ascertaining that employers provide their employees a place of employment free from recognized hazards that are causing or are likely to cause death or serious harm to their employees.

Out of Square

A square or rectangle with corners that are not at 90° angles.

Overfire

To fire glass at a higher heat than intended.

Overglaze

A material containing low melting, finely ground glass, applied to and fired on glass to prevent devitrification.

Overlay

Application of a thin coat of glass over the principal glass.

Ox Hair

Hair taken from the inside of the ears of cattle and frequently used in tracing and matting brushes.

Oxidation

Surface coloring or deterioration caused by exposure to oxygen in the air or to a chemical substance which produces the same effect.

Oxide

Metallic compounds used for coloring glass.

Paint (for glass)

A mixture of finely ground glass, metallic oxides and a liquid mixing agent, such as water and gum arabic, used for painting on glass. It has to be fired for permanent adhesion. See also *Enamel, Grisaille and Silver Stain.*

Painting

Application of color detail or shading to the surface of glass.

Paint Mill

A small mixing unit used to incorporate an oil vehicle with ceramic color.

Palette

A piece of plate glass with a sandblasted or roughened surface on which paint is mixed.

Palette Knife

A very flexible knife-shaped steel blade with no cutting edge for mixing paint.

Palladian Window

A window with three panels, the center panel being wider with an arched top.

Panel

Unit of stained glass leaded together and made to fit an opening in the framework of a window. May be of any shape.

Paperweight

A glass sphere enclosing a decorative element.

Parallax

The seeming displacement of an object by reason of a change in the observer's position.

Parallel

Two or more equidistant lines or planes.

Patching Cement

A material used to repair the walls of a kiln.

Pate de Verre

A process whereby crushed glass is fused in a mold in the kiln.

Patina

A surface treatment on lead or solder to color or age it.

Pattern

A guide or template for cutting the exact design of a piece of glass.

Pattern Shears

Three-bladed scissors which cut a thin strip of paper the width of the lead heart allowing for the width of the came heart between the glass pieces.

Peaked Out

In sand carving, or abrasive etching, the line element of a design resulting in deep V-cuts.

Peephole

A small hole in a kiln with a plug which can be removed for observation.

P.E.L.

See *Permissible Exposure Level.*

Perimeter

The outer boundary of any plane.

Permissible Exposure

The maximum concentration permitted by law; level set by O.S.H.A. of a hazardous material that will have no harmful effects on a person working a standard eight hour day.

Permissible Exposure Limit

An exposure limit established by O.S.H.A. regulatory authority. May be a time-weighted average (TWA) limit on a maximum concentration exposure limit. (See *Time Weighted Average*)

Photo-sensitive Glass

A type of glass where the development of images is dependent upon exposure to ultraviolet radiation and later heat treatment.

Pickle

An acid and water mixture used for cleaning.

Pig

Y-shaped support for the blowpipe. See *Yoke.*

Pigment

A natural or synthetic substance that imparts color.

Pin Holes

A defect consisting of small holes on a glaze or glass.

Pits

Holes in the surface of the glass, generally circular and beginning as clusters of pinpoints, eventually enlarging so that they fuse as the glass corrodes.

Pivoted Window

A window that swings open on pivots at the top and bottom.

Placque (Planche)

A flat piece of screening or perforated metal on which work rests in the kiln.

Plastic

Synthetic resins capable of being molded, shaped or cast, frequently by the use of heat and pressure.

Plasticine

A non-hardening modeling clay.

Plate Glass

Clear window glass that exceeds 3/16″ in thickness

Plating

1. Putting a second piece of glass over a portion of a panel to alter the color, or for reinforcing old glass. Also called *doubling*. 2. Electroplating the lead or solder with nickel or copper, which gives the lead line a bright shine.

Plique à Jour

An enameling technique similar to cloisonné with the metal base that lets light pass through, creating a miniature stained glass window.

Plumbism

See *Lead Poisoning*.

Points

Small flat triangles of zinc used to hold glass in a wooden window sash.

Polariscope

A polarized light device to detect stress in glass. See *Stressometer*.

Polishing

The final smoothing of glass after grinding.

Polyester

A type of monofilament thread used to make silkscreens.

Polyester Epoxy

Generic name for various synthetic resins or plastics.

Pounce Bag

A cloth bag filled with whiting used as a stencil to mark a pattern on glass.

Pontil

A solid iron rod used to hold and manipulate molten glass. See *Punty*

Pontil Scar

The mark or scar where the pontil was attached to the glass. Also *Punty Mark*

Porous

Capable of absorbing liquids.

Ports

In a glass furnace, any opening through which flames or fuel enter or from which exhaust gases escape.

Pot Life

The available working time between mixing a catalyst to resin and it turning hard.

Pot Metal

A molten glass batch of colored glass.

Predella

The small lower section of a window.

Presbytery

The east end of the church housing the alter.

Press

A machine equipped with a mold and plunger for forming glass.

Pressed Glass

Glass that is placed in a mold when hot and pressed into the mold shape.

Pressure Pot

A pressure tank used in a sandblasting system where sand is injected from the tank into the air line.

Primary Colors

Red, yellow, and blue.

Printy

A concave area on glass.

Project

Specific plan, design, or work.

Prunt

A seal or blob of glass applied to a vessel.

P.S.I.

Pounds per square inch, the standard measurement for air pressure.

Pulmonary Edema

This occurs when lungs and air sacs are injured, and the injured tissue pours out a fluid derived from the blood stream interfering with oxygen exchange.

Pumice

A porous form of volcanic glass used as an abrasive.

Punty

A solid iron rod used to hold and manipulate molten glass. See *Pontil*.

Putty

A compound used to seal the glass in the came. Originally a mixture of red lead, whiting, lamp black, and linseed oil. By filling the space between the glass and the lead cames, a weatherproof panel results. At the present time these emulsions often are composed of vegetable and resin oils combined with whiting. Often synthetic thiokols are used today.

Pyrex

Trade name for borosilicate glass that is thermal shock resistant.

Pyrometer
An instrument for measuring temperature in a kiln.

Pyrometric Cone
Small pyramids of shaped ceramic material that bend at a predetermined heat. related to kiln temperature.

Quarries
Diamonds or rectangles of glass leaded together in a lattice design.

Quatrefoil
Small opening in Gothic tracery having four arched sides. Also called *arabesque.*

Quill
1. A feather shaft cut to scratch out lines of paint. 2. A fine squirrel hair brush which uses a quill as a ferrule.

Quill Work
Lines of variegated width that are scratched in glass paint using a quill. Quill work is often used to depict hair.

Rabbet
An 'L' cut all around the perimeter of the window frames, against which the stained glass panels are installed.

Radiant Heat
Heat emitted by a glowing hot element as in a kiln.

Rapid Cool
The third stage in the fusing cycle when the glass is cooled from the fusing temperature to the optimum annealing temperature.

Rapid Heat
The second stage in the fusing cycle when the glass is heated from the strain point to the fusing point.

Raw Batch
A glass charge without cullet.

Realistic
Said of a work of art striving to portray reality.

Reamy
Full antique glass with cords of wavy, irregular surface and large bubbles.

Rebound
Heat returned to the kiln in the cooling process from the brick, insulation, or shelf.

Red Sable
Hair taken from the red sable, a marten-like mammal of Siberia. It is of the highest quality, being springy and yet strong. It is used in liners and tracers.

Reducing Atmosphere
An atmosphere which contains a comparatively small amount of oxygen.

Reed Glass
Clear commercial glass with half circle ribs (refrigerator shelf glass).

Reflected Light
Light being reflected off the surface of glass as opposed to transmitted light.

Refraction
Diffusion or bending of light rays as they are transmitted through a transparent material.

Refractory
A material used to resist the action of heat.

Registration
The use of marks as a guide for printing screened images precisely where intended. Especially necessary when printing more than one color.

Reglet
A 'U' shaped groove in wood or stone used for setting a window.

Reinforcing Rod
Galvanized steel rods or bars used to prevent a stained glass window from sagging or bowing. See *Bar, Saddle Bar.*

Relief
The projection of forms from a flat background.

Renaissance
The reintroduction of classical styles in the 15th and 16th centuries.

Repoussé
A pattern pushed up from the reverse side.

Reredos
The screen at the back of the alter.

Resin
A reactive liquid material which, upon the addition of a catalyst for activation, becomes a solid.

Resistance Wire
Wire that resists the passage of electric current through it, and consequently becomes hot.

Resist Material
Covering used to protect areas to be left unchanged when etching or sandblasting.

Respirator
A mask covering the nose and mouth to prevent inhaling toxic vapors or dust.

Reverse Painting
See *Negative Painting.*

Rheostat
An instrument regulating the strength of an electric current by controlling the amount of resistance.

Rhine
The rolled edge on a glass sheet.

Rigger
A long thin red sable brush used for applying trace lines.

Ring Mottled
Opaque glass with spots of a translucent color. See *Cat's Paw.*

Ripple Glass
Machine-rolled glass, the rippled texture of which is imprinted from the roller.

Rock Crystal
Quartz material used for sandblasting.

Rod
A thin cylindrical length of glass.

Rolled Edge
The edge formed on a piece of glass when the hot glass edge tends to seek an approximate thickness of ¼ ".

Rolled Glass
Sheet glass formed by a roller flattening the glass into sheets.

Romanesque
A style founded on Roman principles, most prevalent in architecture in western Europe from the ninth through the twelfth centuries.

Rondel (Roundel)
Round spun disk of stained glass with a punty mark in the center.

Rose Window
A circular window divided by tracery, usually on the large west wall of a cathedral.

Rouge
Ferric oxide used for polishing.

Roughing
1. The act of creating a course, irregular surface in preparation for finishing and polishing. 2. The first stage of the beveling process, the creation of an angle by abrasive action.

Roving
Bundles of spun glass threads.

Run
The breaking of the glass along the score line.

Running Pliers
Special pliers that push up on the score line and down on either side controlling the breaking of the glass.

S.A.
Semi-antique glass.

Saddle Bar
A metal bar attached to the inside of a stained glass panel and secured to the window jambs to prevent bulging or sagging, or secondary structural elements set into the window frame and attached to the window panels by solder and copper wires to provide additional bracing and support. (See *Bar, Reinforcing Rod*)

Safety Glass
Laminated or annealed glass that, when broken, does not have sharp edges.

Sagging
The downward bending of glass in a mold due to heating. See *Slumping, Bending*.

Sanctuary
The area of the church where the altar is located.

Sandblasting
The technique of blowing sand (or other abrasive materials) under pressure onto the glass surface to etch away part of the glass. See *Abrasive Etching*.

Sand Carving
Abrasive etching done deeper and in layers, creating a sculptural effect.

Sandstone
A natural smoothing stone, consisting chiefly of quartz sand.

Sash
The window frame.

Score
To make a 'cut' line on the surface of the glass with a glass cutter in preparation for breaking it. See *Cutting Glass*.

Score Line
A fracture line made by the glass cutter. See *Fracture*.

Scratching
Creating highlights with a needle (or similar instrument) by removing portions of paint on glass not yet fired. Also called stick work.

Scrubs
Brushes with the bristles cut short and burned, used to remove matting paint before firing.

Scum
Unmelted materials floating on the molten glass.

Sealant
Compound used to seal and fill a joint or opening.

Secondary Colors
Violet, orange and green.

Section
Single panel of a larger stained glass window.

Seeds
Tiny bubbles that add sparkle to the glass.

Seedy Glass
Glass that has tiny bubbles throughout.

Segment
A separate part.

Selenium Colors
The amber, orange, or red colors in glass created by the metallic element selenium.

Semi Antique Glass
Machine drawn transparent glass made to imitate the look of antique glass. Also called *D.A., S.A., G.N.A., F.N.A. and New Antique*.

Separator
High grade shelf primer that glass does not stick to. See *Alumina Hydrate, Kiln Wash, Shelf Primer*.

Servitor
The craftsman in the glass blowing process who takes the molten glass from the gatherer and continues the forming.

Setting
The action of a compound as it becomes more firm.

Shading
Darkening the glass to limit the amount of light transmitted.

Shard
A fragment of broken glass.

Shear Mark
A cooling scar on glass from cutting tools.

Sheet Glass
Flat glass.

Shelf Life
The length of time stored materials remain usable.

Shelf Primer
A material used to cover kiln shelves to keep the glass from sticking. See *Alumina Hydrate, Kiln Wash.*

Shims
All blocks used as spacers in installing a window.

Shop
The team consisting of a gaffer and his helpers that work together around one furnace. There may be many of these 'shops' in a glass house.

Shuttering
The wooden sides of a mold or frame used for casting.

S.I.C.
Standard Industrial Classification.

Sight Line
That point where glass meets and is covered by the lead in a panel, especially at the outside perimeter.

Silica
A mineral used in the manufacture of glass. Also known as sand or silicon dioxide, it is a form of quartz and is used in the manufacture of glass. As a dust, it is extremely hazardous and can cause silicosis.

Silicate
A salt of silicic acid. Many rocks and minerals are silicates. This must be distinguished from *silica,* which is quartz or pure silica. Silicates are non-hazardous.

Silicate of Soda
Water glass, used as an adhesive. See *Sodium Silicate.*

Silicon Carbide
A black water-absorbing mineral known under the trade name of Carborundum, used as an abrasive in engraving and sandblasting, and a principle abrasive used in the beveling process.

Silicosis
Degenerative lung disease caused by inhaling silica dust.

Silk
The fine, strong, lustrous fiber produced by the silk worm, and used for weaving into fabric. The silk thread used in silkscreens for printing is a multi-filament fiber as opposed to a monofilament fiber when nylon, polyester, or wire is used.

Silkscreening
A printing method of applying paint to glass.

Silver Stain
A mixture containing silver salts, which when fired on glass, sinks into the glass, causing a permanent color ranging from pale yellow to amber. See *Amber Stain.*

Single Glazed
The use of a single thickness of glass in a window.

Single Hung
Window that has a stationary top and a moveable bottom half.

Single Strength
Window glass $\frac{1}{16}''$ thick.

Sinter
To fire to the point where cohesion of the glass begins.

Size of the Bead
Width and depth of the solder bead.

Sketch
The preliminary scale drawing of a design.

Slab Glass
Transparent stained glass cast one inch thick. See *Dalle de Verre, Faceted Glass.*

Slider
Window that slides horizontally in the frame.

Slip
Liquid clay.

Slumping
The downward bending of glass into a mold by heating in a kiln.

Slurry
A thin watery mixture.

Smoothing
The second stage of the beveling process, the smoothing of the rough surface.

Soak
The holding of the kiln temperature for a time at a specific range. See *Heat Soak.*

Soaking
To hold the temperature of the kiln constant for a time as it goes through the cooling phase.

Soda Lime Glass
Common glass used for window glass and glassware; flint glass.

Sodium Silicate
Water glass, used as a binder. See *Silicate of Soda.*

Soft Brick
A porous refractory used in kilns.

Softening Point
A transition temperature zone where glass begins to display characteristics of a liquid and will sag under its own weight. Also, the top of the annealing range.

Solder

A metal alloy, generally of tin and lead that when melted will join two intersecting leads together.

Soldering

The act of joining two lead or copper foil pieces together.

Soldering Iron

A heating tool used to solder.

South Side

The south or right side of a church is traditionally the side of Light and the New Testament, which is often reflected in the subject matter and colors of these windows. It is not necessarily compass south.

Spacers

Small blocks placed on the side of a panel to center the window in the opening when installing. (*Shims*)

Spandrel Glass

Heat strengthened float glass with a colored coating. It cannot be recut.

Spatula

A flexible tool with a long, flat blade.

Spectrum

Band of individual colors that results when a beam of light is broken into its component wave lengths of hues.

Spider

A ring with three or four rods that connect the lamp to the lamp shade.

Spray Gun

An apparatus for spraying paint by atomizing the liquid color with compressed air.

Spring Line

The horizontal line below which the upright sides end and the curve of the arch begins.

Squeegee

A rubber blade that forces color through the silk screen.

Squeegee Oil

Oil used to prepare enamels for silkscreening and fusing.

Squirrel Hair

Hair taken from the tails of squirrels, used for the softest brushes for painting. Sometimes called pure camel hair, or mixed with pony hair to form camel hair, or mixed hair. See *Camel Hair.*

Stain

A preparation of silver salts that stains the glass yellow. See *Silver Stain.*

Stained Glass

Glass that is colored during manufacture with metal oxides, cut into a design, and assembled to make a window or other object. See *Leaded Glass.*

Stationary Stop

The permanent stop or lip of the window sash that holds the panel in place.

Stencil

A sheet of heavy paper or metal cut out and used in the repetition of a design.

Stencil Material

Material used as a resist in sandblasting, painting, and silkscreening.

Stippling

A technique for texturing in small dots, and thus shading the glass when matting. There are three types of stippling. wet, applied, and dry, using either the badger blender or a special stippling brush.

Stone

An imperfection in glass, made of non-glassy material.

Stop

Wood or metal flange used to hold a window in place.

Stopgap

The use of glass from another source, often obviously mismatched, to fill a missing piece in a window.

Stopping Knife

A curved, dull bladed knife used to lift the glass from below when leading.

Strain Point

The lower limit of the annealing range.

Strata

Two or more layers.

Streaky

Having a color or colors unevenly distributed in sheet glass to form streaks or swirls.

Strength of Glass

Refers to the thickness of glass, i.e. single or double strength.

Stress

Tension or compression within glass caused by inadequate annealing or incompatible glass.

Stressometer

A light source, a diffusing lens, and two polarized lens that will give a visual reading of stress in glass. See *Polariscope.*

Striations

Surface irregularities that give the glass a crystalline look.

Striking

The change in color that some glass will experience when being reheated. See *Colloidal Colors.*

Stringer Glass

Cathedral glass with thin glass fibers on one side. Also called *streamer glass.* See *Confetti Glass.*

Stringers

Threads pulled from molten glass. Also called *streamers.*

Subsurface

The underside of a sheet of glass.

Sulphide

A cameo incrustation cased with clear glass to form a paperweight or glass object.

Suncatchers
Small glass objects made to hang in windows.

Superimpose
To place one thing upon another.

Support Bars
Iron bars tied to the leaded panel by copper wire for reinforcing. See *Bar, Reinforcing Bar, Saddle Bar.*

Surface
The upper face of a sheet of glass.

Suspension
The dispersion of particles in a liquid.

Symbolism
A sign or image that represents something or someone other than itself.

Siphon Blaster
Sandblaster into which the sand is fed by means of a vacuum from a compressor.

Tack Fire
1. Fusing two objects just to the point where they adhere to each other. 2. Firing glass paint to a point below maturing, but bonded enough to add another layer of paint.

Tack Solder
Applying occasional small amounts of solder to a copper foil project to hold it together.

Tacky
Sticky.

Tangent
Touching but not crossing.

Tapping
Tapping the glass score line from the opposite side to break the glass.

T Bar
Metal 'T' shaped mullions put into a frame opening to support glass panels that will be set one above the other. The T bars receive the weight of each panel and transfer it to the frame.

Temperature
The intensity of heat, measured in degrees Fahrenheit or Centigrade.

Tempered Glass
Flat glass that has been heat treated and abruptly chilled in order to harden and give it extreme toughness for safety reasons.

Template
An exact shape pattern used as a guide for cutting glass.

Tesserae
Small square pieces of glass used in mosaics.

Texture
Uneven surface of glass.

Thermal
Pertaining to heat.

Thermal Shock
Cracking caused by uneven rapid heating or cooling of glass.

Thermocouple
A device used to measure temperature.

Thermoplastic
Plastic materials which soften when heated and harden when cooled.

Thermoset
Plastic materials which harden with heat and cannot be softened again.

Thiokol
A synthetic sealant.

Threshold Limit Value
Concentration of hazardous materials at a level which have no harmful effects upon a person working a standard eight hour day. These are published by the ACGIH and are guides and suggested levels without the force of law. When O.S.H.A. uses one of them as its criteria and makes it a Permissible Exposure Level (*P.E.L.*), then it has the force of law.

Thumb Wax
A soft mixture of beeswax, oil, cornstarch, and rosin used to secure glass pieces to a glass easel. Some plasticine products are also used.

Tie Wires
Copper wires soldered to the panel and twisted around a saddle bar.

Tiffany Lamps
Stained glass lamp shades manufactured by Louis Comfort Tiffany. Now, most foiled lamp shades are called Tiffany lamp shades.

Time Weighted Average (TWA)
The amount of hazardous material collected per cubic meter of air in a measured amount of time averaged over an eight hour day. This takes into account the fact that most hazardous substance exposure is uneven and the *TWA* gives a figure for total exposure in a day regardless of the rate of exposure at any given time.

Tinning
To float solder over a copper foiled surface, a vase cap for a lamp, or top of a soldering iron.

Tin Side
The side of float glass which was in contact with the molten tin bath. This side of the plate or window glass makes gold-base transparent enamels such as rubies and carmines orangy or brownish, and lightens the yellow of silver stains. See *Float Plate Glass.*

Tinted Glass
A mineral mixture incorporated in or on the glass to reduce radiant transmittance.

T.L.V.
See *Threshold Limit Value.*

Total Body Burden
The total amount of lead in the body from all sources, including exposure incidental to the everyday environment.

Toxic Dust Respirators
Respirators rated as acceptable for toxic dusts are suitable for use with paints. In order to wear a respirator, a person must be fitted properly and must be advised by a physician as to whether he can physically accept its restrictions on his breathing.

Toxic Material
A material with the potential to cause adverse health effects. See *Hazardous Material.*

Tracer
Brush for painting trace lines on glass.

Tracery
The stone framework in a gothic window.

Tracing
Using a pointed brush and paint mixed with a liquid to trace onto a piece of clear glass the image of a drawing placed under the glass.

Traditional Design
Motifs and styles handed down from one generation to another.

Training Program
Employers must establish a training and information program for employees exposed to hazardous chemicals in their work area, or exposed to lead above the action level.

Trammel
An instrument for drawing circles or ellipses.

Transept
The transverse section of a church crossing the main nave.

Translucent
Semitransparent, allowing the passage of light but not permitting a clear view.

Transmitted Light
Light that passes through transparent or translucent glass.

Transom Window
A window above a door.

Transparent
Admitting the passage of light with a clear view beyond.

Transparent Colors
Generally known as enamels to stained glass painters, these are extremely transparent, low firing paints which do not have much acid or alkali resistance.

Trefoil
1. A small opening in Gothic tracery having three arcs. 2. A garland design with three loops.

Triptych
A picture, carving, etc. with three parts.

Trivet
A pronged metal support for holding pieces in the kiln.

Tungsten Carbide
Hard metal alloy used for tools.

Tusche
Liquid used to apply a design to a silk screen.

T.W.A.
See *Time Weighted Average.*

Tympanum
The triangular space above a door, sometimes containing a window.

Ultraviolet
Rays of light with a wave length shorter than those of visible light, at the violet end of the spectrum.

Undercoat
A fired coat of enamel over which additional coats of enamel will be fired.

Under Cut
A plane that slants inward in a mold that will prevent the cast glass from being removed.

Underfire
Glass fired at too low a temperature for the desired results.

Unit
One single light of insulation glass.

Value
Quality of lightness or darkness of a color.

Vase Cap
Round brass fitting that goes on top of a lamp shade to hold it to the spider or chain loop.

Vehicle
Oils, spirits, etc. used in the mixing of paints.

Vellum
High quality tracing paper.

Vent
Allowing the escape of fumes through an opening in the kiln.

Vesica, Vesica Pisces
Pointed oval form of aureole.

Vice
A device for holding objects.

Vignette
A picture that shades off gradually into the surrounding ground.

Viscosity
Internal resistance of a liquid to flow.

Viscous
Thick liquid.

Vitreous
Consisting of or resembling glass.

Vitreous Paint
A mixture of ground glass and metallic oxides used to paint on glass. See *Glass Paint.*

Glossary

Vitrified
Converted into glass.

Volatile
Readily and quickly changed into vapor or gas.

Warm Colors
Red, orange, yellow and variants.

Warp
A slight twist or bend in a straight or flat form.

Wash
A thin coat of paint.

Water Glass
1. Sodium silicate that can be used as a medium for glass paints. 1. A type of glass having a texture resembling the gentle ripple of water.

Waxing Up
Sticking pieces of glass on the glass easel with drops of beeswax.

Weathering
The action of the elements in altering color, texture, or form of an exposed object. (In stained glass it has come to mean interior as well as exterior decomposition; for instance, decomposition caused by condensation or fungus.)

West End
The west or entrance end of the church is the people's area. Usually the large west wall has the rose window. It is not necessarily compass west.

Wet Belt
A machine that smoothes the edge of the glass by an abrasive belt.

Wet Blanket
A flexible molding material for high firing. The material is a fiber and has a liquid additive which hardens when air dried.

Whetstone
See *Carborundum Stone.*

Whipping
The action of fanning paint with the badger brush.

White Glass
Term often misused for clear glass.

Whiting
Calcium carbonate—a white powder used as a separator in a kiln, or to clean putty off glass.

Window
An architectural opening in a wall.

Window Glass
Clear glass.

Wire Cloth
A metal cloth which comes in different meshes used for screening.

Wire Glass
Clear glass with a wire mesh embedded in it, so the glass will not shatter when broken.

Wire Screen
Printing screens made out of wire cloth in the same manner in which they are made out of silk, nylon, or polyester.

Wispy
Cathedral glass containing white cloud-like streaks. See *Cloudy Glass.*

Worden System
Brand name for sectional styrofoam forms used to make Tiffany style lamp shades.

Working Range
The period when the glass is cool enough to gather out of the furnace, yet hot enough to work.

Yoke
Y shaped support for the blowpipe. See *Pig.*

Z Section
A Z shaped metal extrusion found as the perimeter of the sash.

Made in the USA
Las Vegas, NV
03 November 2024

10967159R00039